Pennsylvania's Haunted ~Route 22~

By

Ed Kelemen

Copyright © 2014 Ed Kelemen

All rights reserved.

ISBN:1500494828
ISBN-13: 9781500494827

All illustrations and photographs in this book, with the exception of the image of Evelytn Nesbitt on page 70, are the original work of the author.

Cover art by Linda Ciletti

Published in the United States
Nemeleke Publishing
New Florence, Pennsylvania
2014

DEDICATION

This book is dedicated to all those hardy folk, especially my good friends, psychics Bev LaGorga and Patty Wilson, who enter spooky places to meet and help those spirits who, for one reason or another, haven't been able to detach themselves from this earthly plane. Likewise, it is dedicated to the spirits who have been unable to cross over, may they find the peace, serenity, and solace they deserve.

TABLE OF CONTENTS

Acknowledgments
Introduction
About Ghosts and Hauntings
The Ubiquitous Lady In White

Section I
Western Pennsylvania

1. Point State Park..1
2. U.S. Courthouse and Post Office................................7
3. Heinz History Center..11
4. Church Brew Works..17
5. Carnegie Library Lawrenceville..................................20
6. St. Francis/Childrens' Hospital....................................24
7. Clayton..28
8. Roaming Rosie of Restland Cemetery.....................33
9. Wendy's Restaurant at Murrysville..........................36
10. Lessig Cemetery...38
11. Time Travel Civil War Soldier of New Alexandria.42
12. Livermore and Livermore Cemetery........................46
13. Torrance State Hospital...51

Section II
The Allegheny Mountains

14. The Repentant Lover of Packsaddle Gap................56
15. The Horse Thief of Armagh......................................62
16. Ghostly Advice from the Lady in White..................65
17. The Haunt of Eliza Furnace......................................67
18. Elmhurst Mansion..70
19. Lemon House at the Portage Railroad.....................76
20. Ghosts of the Bennington Curve Disaster...............79
21. The Horseshoe Curve...82
22. The Ghost of Buckhorn Mountain..........................86
23. Mishler Theater...88
24. Altoona Railroaders Memorial Museum.................92
25. Baker Mansion..95
26. Lakemont Amusement Park..................................100

Section III
The Juniata River Valley

27. U. S. Hotel..104
28. Royer Mansion...109
29. The Feed Mill Infant Ghost....................................112
30. Inn at Edgewater Acres..114
31. Gypsy Wild's House...117
32. Lewistown Haunts...119
33. General "Mad" Anthony Wayne's Bones.............123
34. Amity Hall Hotel..128

Section IV
Harrisburg and the Hex Highway

35. Lunatic Asylum of Pennsylvania..........................134
36. Pennsylvania Bar Association(Maclay Mansion)..139
37. Hex Highway..141
38. Charming Forge Mansion..................................143
39. Shartlesville Hotel..146
40. Schuylkill River at Hamburg.............................149
41. Hawk Mountain..152
42. Maple Grove Inn..158
43. Magnolia's Restaurant...................................161

Section V
Allentown and The Lehigh Valley

44. Ressurection Cemetery..................................166
45. Dorney Park...168
46. King George Inn..172
47. Cedar Crest College.....................................175
48. Muhlenberg College......................................177
49. The Hamilton Street Ghost.............................180
50. Constitution Drive.......................................182
51. Roxy Theater..184
52. Lehigh University Linderman Library.................186
53. Anna Mia's Restaurant..................................189
54. Moravian Book Shop.....................................191
55. Historic Hotel Bethlehem...............................193
56. Sun Inn..200
57. Moravian College..202
58. Heckewelder's Ghost....................................208

VI
Eastern Pennsylvania

59. Indian Tower..214
60. Whitefield House..217
61. Newburg Inn..220
62. Easton Library...223
63. State Theater...226
64. Getter Ghosts..229
65. Stemies/Black Horse Tavern.............................232

Visiting the Ghosts of Route 22..............................236

About the Author...243

Other Books by Ed Kelemen....................................244

ACKNOWLEDGMENTS

There are just so many people to thank who have made this book possible.

My undying gratitude goes to the countless people of Pennsylvania who have, over the past few centuries, taken the time to pass down their experiences and stories of the paranormal events that they experienced. And to those stalwart souls who have taken the time to verify the stories and separate the folklore from the actual events.

Thanks to Mary Ann Mogus for getting me started on this project about Pennsylvania's haunted highways, and to my wonderful wife, Lynnie, for lighting a fire under my butt to get the book completed.

Thanks to the members of the Greensburg Writers Group, the world's most gentle critique group for all the support that this bunch of extremely talented writers have given me.

I extend my heartfelt gratitude to those who have allowed me to share their otherworldly experiences with you:

Thank you Maxine Ruble for sharing your family's experiences with the ghosts who had wandered away from the nearby cemetery. Marge Burke, thank you for your wonderful story about the Civil War soldier who, after 150 years, is still trying to get home from the war. To Joan Grimes Kowalski, thank you for your permission to reprint your award-winning poem, "The White Lady of the Buckhorn," about the young bride to be who lost her life searching for her fiancee who was lost in a blinding snowstorm and searches for him still to this day. And again I thank you Joan Grimes Kowalski for allowing me to use your poem that catches the essence of Evelyn Nesbitt's haunting of Elmhurst Mansion, simply titled, "Evelyn of Elmhurst."

>*<

Special thanks goes to Judith Gallagher of Gallagher's Editorial Services whose red editorial pen has made this book a readable entity. Any grammatical errors and typos that occur in this book are as a result of printing gremlins that snuck in uninvited and are my fault alone.

>*<

The incomparable cover art is by Linda Ciletti, a graphic artist beyond compare. Visit with her at www.lindaciletti.net for a visit and a chance to admire additional examples of her work.

INTRODUCTION

Route 22 in Pennsylvania

Route 22 is also called the William Penn Highway after the founder of the Commonwealth of Pennsylvania. The word Pennsylvania actually translates into "Penn's Woods." However, it could as well be called the Schizophrenic Highway. It started off not knowing where it wanted to go. Oh, it knew it wanted to go in an easterly-westerly direction, but that was about it. It was undecided whether it wanted to run through Philadelphia, Allentown, Pittsburgh, or New Castle. So, at one time or another, it ran through all of them. With such a penchant for wanderlust, it is no surprise that lost souls wander its length to this day.

In 1914, a group met in St. Joseph, MO and proposed a national route from New York City to San Francisco. It was called the Pikes Peak Ocean to Ocean (PPOO) Highway. This highway was to follow a portion of the National Old Trails Road through Philadelphia, Baltimore, Washington, Cumberland, and Wheeling in its eastern leg. Strangely, there was no mention of New York City in this incarnation. That was rectified on February 15th, 1916 when an independent alignment east of St. Louis was adopted. This called for its eastern end to run through Pittsburgh, to Johnstown and Altoona. Then on through Harrisburg to Pottstown and Philadelphia. A connecting branch was to run South from Harrisburg to Washington,. DC and North from Reading, PA to New York City. The route didn't have a number yet and it was already running all over Pennsylvania.

The William Penn Highway Association of Pennsylvania tried to fix that on March 27, 1916 when 650 of their members met at an auditorium in Harrisburg to propose a new West to East route that would, "parallel the Pennsylvania Railroad and offer an alternative to the Lincoln Highway between Pittsburgh and Philadelphia." There would also be a New York extension running from Allentown, through Bethlehem and Easton in Pennsylvania. The group published a brochure in November of that year explaining that their aim was, "the permanentization of an arterial road system in Pennsylvania generally, and the William Penn Highway in particular." What happened to the Harrisburg to New York route? Never fear, it shall return.

Anyhow, not much happened during the next 10 years with the PPOO Highway. People in Pennsylvania went along with their own design and implementation of the William Penn Highway. You see, in 1923 a law was passed in Harrisburg that gave the Secretary of Highways the sole authority to name or number Pennsylvania's roads. This was to prevent confusion about a road's name as it traveled throughout the various communities of the state.

One of the first things the Secretary of Highways at that time did was to designate the Lincoln Highway as PA Route #1. At that time named roads in the Commonwealth included Lincoln Highway, William Penn Highway, Lackawanna Trail, Susquehanna Trail, Roosevelt Highway, Lakes-to-Sea Highway, National Pike, Baltimore Pike, and the Chicago to Buffalo Highway, all in Pennsylvania. See how that prevented confusion?

The William Penn Highway was to be called Route 3 and would run from Pittsburgh to Easton in the Northeast end of the State on its way to New York City. Along that route it ran through Blairsville, Ebensburg, Cresson, Hollidaysburg, Lewistown, Harrisburg, Lebanon, Reading, and Allentown.

A couple of years later the American Association of State Highway Officials, appropriately enough going under the acronym AASHO, approved its own numbering system and designated that highway as U.S. Route 22. There were also six branches of that highway numbered U.S. Routes 122, 222, 322, 422, 522, and 622.

The PA State Secretary of Highways, William Connell basically said in a letter of January 28, 1927, "Oh, no no no, we didn't agree to anything like that."

In February of that same year, John Macfall of AASHO replied saying, "Oh yes, yes, yes you did."

There was a bunch of letters following that that said PA didn't like the Federal numbering system of even numbers for east-west and odd Numbers for north-south highways. And that the State wanted to keep using its own numbers as well as federal numbers. Then it said that it wanted to just use federal numbers, then just state numbers. Then there was a telegram saying that a decision would be made in March. Then there were notes, telegrams, and letters saying, "OK, we'll do it your way," sent between the state and the federal highway people.

This went on and on and on with Pennsylvania and AASHO arguing all the way up to and through 1936. By 1942 U.S. Route 22 in Pennsylvania covered some 655 miles. Adjustment after adjustment has been made and finally today's route had settled down into a west-east route in 1954 running through Pittsburgh, Blairsville, Ebensburg, Hollidaysburg, Lewistown, Harrisburg, Allentown, and Easton, covering about 315 miles. Since U.S. Route 22 now runs from New York City to Cincinnati, Ohio where it ends, it leaves the unanswered question: Whatever happened to the Pikes Peak Ocean to Ocean highway?

And don't think that Route 22 has settled down just yet. Every time someone has a chance, a bypass is built somewhere along the route that avoids contact with Pennsylvania's rich and varied cultures and forces us onto that interminable concrete ribbon to boredom.

Since Route 22 seems to have meandered all over the state, for this purpose of this book, we are primarily going to concern ourselves with U.S. Route 22 as it exists today, but making detours to travel along what is affectionately called "Old Route 22" and "Old William Penn Highway" by the people who live (and have an afterlife) along it.

I want to take this opportunity to caution you about the directions that I have provided to the haunted locations throughout this book. They were correct when I wrote them. However, sometimes the spirits can be mischievous and they might get the idea to make changes here and there. Those changes could get you lost. So, before actually visiting any of these places, do a reality check and verify that my directions are correct prior to setting out on an adventure.

About Ghosts and Hauntings

Webster says that a ghost is, "the specter of a person appearing after their death, an apparition." A whole bunch of entries later, Webster says that to be haunted is, "to be frequented by ghosts, spirits, etc." If it's good enough for Webster, it's good enough for me. That "etc.," gives me pause, however.

The greatest majority of the hauntings in this book are of the ghostly persuasion. They range from the shades of infants to those of historical figures, and everything in-between. And, the great preponderance of them died in a way that most coroners would not call, "of natural causes."

Webster just tells us, "what," not, "why." For some reason or other, these spirits have unfinished business in this plane of existence. They must accomplish something before they can go on. Maybe there is a message that must be delivered, or a murderer caught, or a warning issued. Some look for their lost children. Many just aren't ready to die. It is a shock to their systems in more ways than one. One thing we can be sure of is that intense emotions are involved.

The locations that are haunted the most tell U.S. that. Where are emotions more intense than in prisons and hospitals where life and death meet each other on a daily basis? How about institutions of higher learning where a person's whole future can hinge on one passing grade? Then there is the compounded shame of a mother whose guilt over murdering her own child causes her to end her own life. How about the emotions generated by lynchings, epidemics, and wholesale slaughter? Robbery and murder, unrequited love and murder, jealousy and murder – is a pattern emerging?

What about that, "etc?" The sounds of phantom horses clip-clopping along the cobblestones, ghostly trains running off the tracks, and ghostly lights all fall into this category.

If there's one thing I've learned during my research into the paranormal, it's that locations where emotions run rampant produce haunts. I can think of at least one place where the ghost was so satisfied in corporeal life and has such happy memories associated with that place, it has decided to stay there. It has no message from beyond the grave other than, "Don't worry – be happy." But, since it is nowhere near Route 22, it isn't in this book.

Now, the only way I can learn about ghosts and their locations is for someone to tell me. Future endeavors along this line will include subsequent editions of, Pennsylvania's Haunted Route 22, Route 30, Route 6, and the coal country of PA. While I cannot afford to pay for stories, anyone who furnishes me with one that gets into print will receive credit in the book for the story and an autographed copy of the book.

I can be contacted at ed@ekelemen.com and you can visit with me at my web site: www.ekelemen.com.

The Ubiquitous Lady in White

I'd like to attempt to clarify something here. Many times, in this book and others, the Lady in White is mentioned. She has been seen in every possible paranormal context. She appears at the side of the road hitch-hiking. She is seen floating in various places and circumstances. The Lady in White walks into a lake and disappears under the merciless waters. She rides along with you in your car only to fade from view as her destination is approached. She flits about cemeteries. She stands alongside and in the middle of roads, next to fences, peers from windows and doorways, and is generally the most seen phantasm.

Are all these appearances of The Lady in White, the same spirit? Of course not.

It takes a tremendous amount of energy for a spirit to manifest itself materially. If there isn't a readily available easily accessed power source present, the spirit will only be able to partially appear. That is why spirits often announce their presence with orbs. Orbs are the least draining manner of appearing, since they are basically featureless and relatively small. Orbs are the most common overt evidence of spirit presence.

Often a spirit only has enough available energy to be able to communicate via EVPs. This is because the digital recording device is present and supplying its own power source in the form of batteries for the spirit to access.

Other energy conserving ways that the spirits interact with us is through the use of Ouija boards, dowsing rods, and pendulums. The person using the object furnishes the energy.

It requires much more energy than most spirits have at their command to appear as a full-bodied apparition. That's what makes full-bodied apparitions so rare. That energy has to come from somewhere and that's why apparitions are accompanied by cold spots. Heat is a form of energy, and it is the most readily-available one. By draining the heat in an area, a spirit can increase his or her available energy, then use that energy to interact with us.

Energy conservation is what it is all about. Projecting an image on a background, such as a mist rather than appearing three dimensionally is one way to do that. Another way is to appear only partially, such as just a head in a window.

A full-bodied, three dimensional appearance is the second most energy draining event that a spirit can accomplish. By appearing in a semi-transparent, monochromatic state the interaction can last longer to achieve the spirit's intent. This monochromatic event is usually in shades of gray, like a black and white photograph. Within gray scales, all light colors appear as though they are faded white.

So, female spirits wearing dresses are often assumed to be wearing white dresses when they appear, thus promulgating the legend of "The Lady in White."

What is the most energy draining way for spirits to interact with us? By moving inanimate objects.

~1~
Western Pennsylvania

Point State Park

Pittsburgh

Route 22, also known as the William Penn Highway, shares its way through the Point area of downtown Pittsburgh with Route 30, the subject of my previous book, *Pennsylvania's Haunted Route 30*. Both books start where the great Ohio River is created by the confluence of the Allegheny and Monongahela rivers at what is now Point State Park.

Pittsburgh's icon, the huge fountain is the focal point of the convergence of the Monongahela and Allegheny rivers to create the mighty Ohio, the nation's first superhighway. It wasn't always so.

As little as 300 years ago the only feet that trod the forested juncture of rivers were encased in moccasins. These belonged to the original people who husbanded and kept the area pristine for over 13,000 years. The first were members of the Mound Builders, then the Hopewell culture. Then came the Iroquois, Lenape, and Shawnee, all tribes that had been displaced by European settlers to the east and south. They had been devastated by the diseases that the Europeans brought with them. It's a small wonder that many of their spirits chose to remain behind rather than infect the after-world with the white man's diseases.

Pittsburgh's first incarnation was a short-lived one as Fort St. George under British rule after then-Major George Washington had politely asked the French military presence to leave the area. A few months later, in April 1754, while the fort was barely half built, 500 Frenchmen returned. They evicted the British settlers who had come from Virginia and built Fort Duquesne on the same spot. But they were able to hold it for only four years. In 1758 General John Forbes retook it from the French, built a new fort there, and christened it Fort Pitt. The spirits of many of the Indians, French settlers, and British settlers who lost their lives in these struggles imbued what would come to be known as the Point District.

This small British foothold at the headwaters of the Ohio River grew and grew. The town that sprang up around the fort was named Pittsburgh. Since it was the jumping-off place for the myriad of pioneers heading into the sunset to settle America, it was called the Gateway to the West. A large industry grew here manufacturing keelboats for those settlers. They traveled the Ohio in those keelboats until they decided to strike westward overland. At that point, they dismantled the keelboats and reassembled them into wagons for the westward trek. On July 15, 1802, Merriweather Lewis and William Clark departed Pittsburgh on their journey of exploration to find a transcontinental water route to the Northwest Territories. By that time, the Point District was a jumble of small manufacturing plants and wharves devoted to the keelboat industry.

Some enterprising souls discovered that the Pittsburgh area was ideally suited for the manufacture of iron. The surrounding mountains were full of ore and the forests of Western Pennsylvania provided the fuel to stoke the furnaces. An inexhaustible supply of coal was discovered in the Appalachian Range, and the rivers were the highways to deliver all these supplies. Pittsburgh was reborn as the Iron City. Its population went from around 1,500 in 1800 to 50,000 in 1860. During his 1842 visit to the city, Charles Dickens described it as "Hell with the lid off." The Point District devolved into a mishmash of warehouses, foundries, brothels, saloons, and derelict hotels. It existed to serve the iron-smelting industry.

Pittsburgh garnered a new nickname during this period. It was derisively called the Smoky City. Two things brought boom times to Pittsburgh: the railroad and the American Civil War. By the war's end, the city of

Pittsburgh was producing more than half of the nation's steel and one-third of the country's glass.

Pittsburgh was reborn again, this time as the Steel City. But the derogatory appellation Smoky City stayed on. Now the Point District was crisscrossed with railroad tracks.

For the next hundred years, things became worse and worse. For the first half of the 20th century, office workers had to bring at least two shirts a day to work because the first shirt would be too coated with soot by noon to present a professional appearance. Lower-echelon clerks brought extra white collars made of stiffened cardboard, and they periodically whitened those collars with chalk during the artificial overcast that passed for daylight. The pollution from the steel mills darkened the skies so much that streetlights had to be kept on all day.

It became apparent that something had to be done. The air was so thick that it could be cut with a knife, and it had a constant malodorous overlay of sulfur dioxide that gave it the essence of rotten eggs that had been consumed with copious amounts of beer, then transformed into methane gas by a human gastric process. Finally, in the 1950s, the governor of Pennsylvania (and past mayor of Pittsburgh), David L. Lawrence, amassed enough political power to do what had to be done. He made it his life's work to eradicate, once and for all, the city's reputation as the Smoky City.

The Point was still a dingy eyesore of slums, warehouses, and derelict buildings. Lawrence wanted to turn it into the Golden Triangle, a showplace of modern skyscrapers, office buildings, and hotels in a park-like setting. He had quite a bit of opposition in this endeavor.

A huge portion of the distressed area was owned by influential people in the city's hierarchy. But Lawrence, along with his banking mogul ally, Richard K. Mellon, steamrolled that opposition. The city acquired property after property by eminent domain and bulldozed them to clear the way for the Golden Triangle.

Finally all that was left to acquire was a small knot of warehouses right in the middle of the area. The owners refused to move. And a fire of "unknown accidental origin" destroyed those buildings one night, and the last impediment to the construction of the Golden Triangle was removed.

The original outlines of the Fort Pitt Blockhouse and bastions were rediscovered. Two double-deck multilane bridges were built linking Pittsburgh with places north and south on newly created interstate highways. And a brand-new park dubbed Point State Park announced Pittsburgh's Renaissance to the world. Its huge fountain washed away the city's identity of soot, grime, and smoke. Chaos gave way to serenity.

The whole area around the blockhouse and the fort is ringed with security cameras. Security officers who monitor those cameras are reluctant to talk about some of the things they see late at night, like people dressed in 19th and early 20th century garb, looking as though they are headed either to or from work. The men swing that emblem of the industrial laborer, the lunch pail. The women, mostly dressed as maids, washerwomen, or cleaners, walk alongside them. Frequent forays to evict these unwanted people from the museum grounds always meet with failure because the trespassers are only seen on the monitors.

A beautiful park in the center of a bustling city attracts other trespassers as well. When the weather is agreeable, the numbers of homeless people increase. On the paths, byways, and undersides of bridge ramps within the park they congregate and exchange stories of the apparitions they've encountered: frontiersmen, George Washington himself, Indians, and indistinct specters in the mists of the riverbanks. The police who are sent to deal with these squatters aren't too fast to discount their stories. More than one officer has also encountered those same spirits of times long gone.

If you find yourself strolling along in the twilight of evening or in the mist of a newly dawned day in the direction of the fountain approaching the bridge overpass, keep your wits about you. You're not imagining that frontiersman leaning against that tree or that 19th century lady hurrying off to work around that bush. You may even encounter the father of our country as he prepares his troops for the retreat to Fort Necessity.

Take a stroll from Point State Park along Liberty Avenue through the gleaming skyscrapers known as Gateway Center. Over there on your left is Gateway Number 1, the home of KDKA Radio, the first commercial radio station in the world. From here, Old Route 22 follows Penn Ave., which just happens to be one-way the opposite way, so we'll go along Liberty Avenue, which has been the way east for the last 40 years or more. When you get to the maniacally designed intersection where Grant Street comes in from the right, look to your right to see the United States Courthouse.

The United States Courthouse & Post Office Building

**700 Grant Street
Pittsburgh**

When Pittsburgh native and multimillionaire Andrew W. Mellon was appointed Secretary of the U.S. Treasury, he allocated funds for the construction of a new Federal Building in Pittsburgh, designed to reflect western Pennsylvania's rise in national political and economic influence. The eleven-story edifice opened in 1934, somberly overshadowing the area. Its no-nonsense stripped classical architecture was intended to convey the stability and dignity of the federal government at that turbulent time, the depths of the Great Depression.

One unusual feature of the building was that a portion of it was built over the rail line to save time transporting the mail between the distribution center in the building and the railroad station. Those railroad tracks are long gone now, but the U.S. Post Office is still in the building, which is located next to the Pennsylvania Railroad Station and across from the William S. Moorehead Federal Building. The Post Office building is seldom noticed by Pittsburgh natives – except on April 15, when postal workers stand curbside on Seventh Avenue until midnight to collect tax returns from the habitual procrastinators that infest every city.

In 1985, the Post Office building was listed in the National Register of Historic Places as part of the Pittsburgh Central Downtown Historic District. Ten years later it received its own listing in the National Register of Historic Places.

The building had been stained by 60 years of grit, soot, and exposure to Pittsburgh's atmosphere, including 25 years of its most toxic industrial smog. In view of these new accolades, it needed a facelift, which included a thorough cleaning of the granite and sandstone exterior and a general sprucing of windows, doors, frames, and the like. Inside, new courtrooms were added and old ones were refurbished.

One of those courtrooms was presided over by Judge Gerald Weber from 1965 to 1988. He had given the cleverly worded decision in a case brought before him in 1971 by one Gerald Mayo. Mr. Mayo was suing Satan and his staff for deliberately placing obstacles in his path, bringing misery and causing Mr. Mayo's downfall by depriving him of his constitutional rights. Judge Weber declined to prosecute the case, noting that Mr. Mayo had not provided adequate instructions on exactly how and where the U.S. Marshal could find Satan to serve process on him.

Judge Weber passed away at his home in Erie, Pennsylvania, in 1989, but he sometimes returns to the U.S. Courthouse on Grant Street to oversee legal proceedings. Perhaps, in his afterlife, he found a way to instruct U.S. Marshals who are no longer part of this mortal coil exactly how to serve process on Satan.

While doing renovation work in the courthouse in 1990, an electrician encountered a black-robed figure roaming between the massive columns. The figure strode up to the worker and asked him, "How's it going?" Then it walked away. Although nonplussed, the electrician remained unruffled – for a while. When an orange figure of indeterminate shape and substance flew over his head later the same evening, he left the building running and screaming to share his experience at one of the many watering holes nearby whilst imbibing that Pittsburgh mainstay of nerve-calming elixir: a shot and a beer. Later the electrician shared his experience with a co-worker. She said that she too had seen the robed figure, and that it was a twin to Judge Weber in the painting of him hanging in the courthouse. Others have witnessed Judge Weber walking to and fro in his judicial robes near his courtroom.

Judge Weber isn't the only specter lingering in the courthouse. Office cleaning staff report seeing a federal director who was no longer of this earth roaming the fourth floor as well. They didn't mention what he was a director of.

Maintenance people have heard disembodied footsteps along the corridors, doors slamming in the offices, voices, and even aggravating spirits calling their names. These things have happened throughout the building, most often on the fourth, first, and ninth floors.

OK, let's put this place in our rear-view mirror and head on east. Again, Penn Avenue is one way the opposite way, so we'll cross Liberty Avenue and Penn Avenue, then turn right onto Smallman Street, which runs upstream along the bank of the Allegheny River and was the direction of Route 22 before anyone ever contemplated a Route 22. It was originally an unpaved street where all of western Pennsylvania's consumable goods were brought to market on horse-drawn wagons from the farms where they originated. All this commercial activity took and still takes place in a 10-block long extra-wide strip of warehouses ending at the front entrance of Saint Stanislavsky Church on 21st Street.

Senator John Heinz History Center

The Strip District
1212 Smallman Street
Pittsburgh

Today it is known as the Strip District, and it is arguably the most schizophrenic urban area in the country. Unlike humans who suffer from this malady, the Strip District revels in it. It is a center of frenetic activity twenty-four hours a day.

Its first personality was its original one as an actual market district. Smallman Street itself was designed to be wide enough that the many horse-drawn wagons could sit three and four deep, whiling away the early hours, as their drivers haggled over the price of the cargo. Nowadays, the huge tractor trailers that jam it during the wee hours have plenty of room to maneuver and wait their turn to back into the many loading docks. Once the late night and early morning hours were filled with the whinnying of horses who stamped their hooves and blew clouds of steam from their nostrils. Today, the waning of night and approach of dawn fill with the burbling of diesel engines and the blue vapor of exhaust from the steel and aluminum beasts of burden who bring the day's produce to market.

Parked next to, in front of, behind, and in between the 53-foot-long trailers and tractors are a myriad of delivery vans and medium-size trucks belonging to the tri-state area's grocery stores, delis, restaurants, and wholesalers.

All this vehicular activity is linked to the loading docks of places with names like Wholey's, Wholesale Produce Industry, Weiss Provisions, Strip District Meats, Consumers Produce Company, Euclid Fish Company, and Parma Sausage Products. All of these locations bustle with hundreds of people vying to get the best products at the best price, to be delivered that same morning before their stores open for business.

By 6:00 a.m., the Strip District is deserted, the only evidence of its earlier coordinated chaos a few scraps of paper fluttering in the morning breeze off the river and one or two warehouse employees still brooming debris from the empty loading docks.

The district undergoes its first personality change as it prepares for the onslaught of daytime occupants drawn to the area by its many trendy coffee shops, delis, and ethnic restaurants wedged side by side with wholesale dealers of every stripe offering discount deals to anyone who walks in the door. If you can't find what you want for wholesale prices in the Strip District during the day, then it just isn't for sale in Pittsburgh. This goes on nonstop all day until the evening rush hour ends and all the workers of downtown Pittsburgh return to their mostly suburban homes.

For a few hours, the Strip District catches its collective breath while all the wholesale-retail outlets close, the sidewalk cafés bring in their tables, and the other occupants bring down their bomb-proof overhead metal doors, once again turning the whole area into a deserted urban canyon.

After the sun sets, neon signs flicker to life one by one. The District transforms yet again, this time into the city's premier nightclubbing destination. Thousands of people, young and old, flock to the Strip District's clubs to enjoy a night of revelry in establishments that specialize in entertainment ranging from jazz to country to hip-hop to salsa and everything in between. All the semis and delivery trucks were replaced with minivans, SUVs, and other commuter conveyances in the morning. Now they are replaced with Acuras, BMWs, and Audis polished within an inch of their lives. And so it goes until the clubs close and the semis rumble toward approaching the warehouses, their trailers full of produce, meat, and seafood.

All these foods must be preserved until they hit the tables of consumers. But refrigerators were neither widely available nor affordable for working families until after the Second World War. Refrigeration was provided by iceboxes, wooden or metal boxes that held a large block of ice in an insulated enclosure with the perishable foodstuffs. One purveyor of this expendable, valuable product was the Chatauqua Lake Ice Company.

The Heinz History Center, is located in the former Chautauqua Lake Ice Company Building at 1212

Smallman Street. The building takes up an entire block between 12th and 13th Streets. That's how much demand there was for ice in the old days. On February 9, 1898, a fire alarm sounded at 7:55 p.m. for a fire at that building. Twelve hours later, 11 people were confirmed dead and 27 were missing, and 19 seriously injured people had been taken to area hospitals. The building had been wracked by fire and explosions fed by ammonia leaks and 800 barrels of whiskey, which had been stored in the building's warehouse. Walls had tumbled, the building was gutted and in ruins.

The building was reconstructed. The Chatauqua Lake Ice Company was back in business serving the ice needs of the area by the end of 1899. It continued to do so well into the 20th century, finally passing out of business in 1953. For the next few years it was used as a lumber storage warehouse. It eventually fell into disuse until it was renovated and reincarnated as the Senator John Heinz History Center. Opened in 1996, it consists of five floors of both permanent and changing exhibits bringing to life the rich and varied history of Pennsylvania.

It is no wonder that the museum has picked up its share of otherworldly figures who just refuse to fade into the dusty confines of history books and insist on existing side by side with the exhibits in the center.

If you wander the exhibits, you may notice a fellow checking out an original Heinz Company horse-drawn delivery wagon. If you see him climb onto the wagon, don't bother to admonish him. He will dissolve and disappear before your eyes before you can get within arm's reach. But if you hear an alarm, you better pay attention to it. It may actually be a real alarm—though it may be set off by unseen occupants who like to "alarm" visitors. Like the fellow who clambers aboard the delivery wagon, other haunts board the Pittsburgh Railways Company streetcar and wait for it to depart on its way along the Drake Line (which of course no longer exists). Maybe that's why they fade from sight. Or is because they don't have 22 cents for the fare?

An article in the *Pittsburgh Post-Gazette* of February 3, 2002, by Lillian Thomas was titled, "Fire, Ice: a Chilling Tale." It quoted workers and staff who'd had experiences with spectral entities wandering about the building, mostly on the fifth floor and the loading dock area.

A long-time security officer working at the building has had many experiences with ghosts, both passive and active. One in particular was fond of switching off lights on a seven-switch panel, one at a time. Another walked into and out of the officer's field of vision, entering the main exhibit area after the museum was closed for the evening.

A paranormal research team from the Mon Valley conducted an investigation at the museum and rated it a 7 on a scale of 10 for paranormal activity.

Over the years, staff and volunteers at the museum have grown comfortable sharing space with the otherworldly denizens who enjoy reliving past experiences in the exhibits. Steve Doell, archivist at the museum, simply puts it this way: "We welcome all visitors."

>*<

Heading east in the Strip District will bring us up short at the front doors of St. Stanislaus, so let's turn right there, cross over Penn Avenue again, and turn left at Liberty Avenue, again paralleling Penn Avenue. After about a half mile, Liberty Avenue veers to the right and starts going uphill.

You will notice on the left side of the street a church beautifully appointed with stained-glass windows. You'll also notice the sign "Church Brew Works." There is no better place to stop for a while, quaff some award-winning handcrafted beer, and satisfy your appetite with chef-inspired and interpreted local and international cuisine. Likewise, there is no better place to rub elbows with a dearly departed man of the cloth.

Church Brew Works

**3525 Liberty Ave.
Pittsburgh**

Well over 100 years ago, in 1878, St. John the Baptist Roman Catholic Parish was founded to serve the needs of people in between Lawrenceville and the Strip District. It quickly outgrew the first building, which housed both the church and school. The Diocese acquired additional property and, in 1903, a new and beautiful church was dedicated on that property. The old church was turned completely into a school building with classrooms where the pews, pulpit, and altars once held sway. When newer and larger Catholic schools opened nearby, the original building was sold. For 90 years, generations of Catholics were baptized, confirmed, married, and buried in the church. Countless happy-faced second-grade children dressed all in gleaming white received their First Holy Communion at its altar.

In 1993, the declining urban population meant that there were too many small independent parishes in the Lawrenceville area. The age of parish consolidation had arrived, and St. John the Baptist was combined with three other parishes were to form Our Lady of the Angels Parish.

Entrepreneur Sean Casey had a vision for the church. He bought it, removed all the environmentally unsafe elements such as asbestos and lead-based paints, remodeled and refurbished, and reopened it in 1996 as the Church Brew Works. It is now one of the country's foremost microbreweries and is equally famous for the quality of its food.

Although some people expressed concern at the prospect of a brewery and restaurant within the confines of a church, it has proved to be a boon to the neighborhood. In fact, Mr. Casey's restoration of the facility was so well done that it was granted Historic Landmark status in 2001 by the Pittsburgh History and Landmarks Foundation. It provides more than 80 full- and part-time jobs to local people and has actually raised the value of local real estate at a time when urban property values were declining.

Be that as it may, there is at least one person who seems dissatisfied with the church's transformation. Pius Monk Dunkel has decided to stay on during his afterlife, looking down on the immaculately gleaming vats producing divine fermentations such as Celestial Gold, Pipe Organ Pale Ale. Visitors spot the priest patrolling the former choir loft, possibly lamenting the loss of earthly voices soaring heavenward where now he is privy to dinner conversations over sumptuous feasts. Speculation has it that he has decided to tend the phantom altar until Judgment Day, overhearing couples' confessions of mutual love rather than transgressions. Or maybe he is just drawn to the conviviality, camaraderie, and good vibes that have continued here unabated since the building hosted St. John the Baptist's Parish.

While we are pausing here to enjoy that good cheer, food, and drinks, let's consider our next stop. A half dozen or so blocks along Liberty Avenue will bring us to Fisk Street. A left on Fisk a few blocks along and we'll cross Penn Avenue and, in the middle of the third block after Penn Avenue is one of many haunted libraries across this state.

Carnegie Library Branch

279 Fisk Street
Pittsburgh

In 1814 the Lawrenceville Burying Ground, or as it was sometimes called, The Washington Burying Ground, was opened for the interment of local townspeople and soldiers who had died while stationed at the Allegheny Arsenal nearby. The ground for the cemetery was donated by the founder of the Borough of Lawrenceville, William Foster. Perhaps you have heard of Mr. Foster's son, Stephen Foster. Over the next 30 years the cemetery served the community well as a final resting place for loved ones. Even after the opening of the huge Allegheny Cemetery nearby, local citizens continued to be buried in their beloved little burying ground.

That, however, all came to an end after the Borough of Lawrenceville was incorporated into the City of Pittsburgh in 1868. You see, the cemetery was considered public lands. So, in 1881, when the school board was looking about for a place to build a new school, this little pastoral piece of solace and comfort came to their attention and was appropriated for that use.

Work commenced early in 1882 on the foundation of the school, and the excavation that ensued was done without regard for the remains of those buried there. Bones and caskets were dug up and cast aside willy-nilly, causing anguish among the relatives left behind. The school board was taken to court by a group of concerned citizens who testified that as many as 500 people were buried there and that the ground had been originally donated expressly for use as a cemetery, not for "educational purposes," as the school board's petition for use had falsely maintained.

An agreement between the school board and the litigants was reached: The 500 bodies would be moved from the Lawrenceville Burying Ground to the Allegheny Cemetery, and what was left of the Lawrenceville Burying Ground would be enclosed with a fence. In 1887, to complete the terms of the settlement, a monument was erected there bearing the inscription, "In honor of the American soldiers buried here. We will emulate their patriotism and protect their remains." It just goes to show that chiseling a sentiment into stone doesn't necessarily make it true.

The people entrusted with the disinterment and

retraction were less than diligent about their duties. About 70 souls never made it to the Allegheny Cemetery. Their bones and caskets kept being unearthed as the workmen continued digging the cellar and foundation and doing miscellaneous landscaping on the site. The remains of these 70 souls were dumped into a mass grave at the edge of the property, where they wouldn't interfere with the construction. At least that was what the contractors thought.

The school was built and named after Stephen C. Foster. It stayed opened until 1939, turning out hundreds, if not thousands, of elementary school graduates into the population of the city.

In 1898, work began on the Carnegie Public Library of Pittsburgh Lawrenceville Branch, also within the confines of the original cemetery's boundaries. The building is still in use and still occupies that location. Workmen eventually refused to work night shifts because of the unearthly moans and groans floating on the night air. The spirits of those who have been refused a proper burial with the respect they deserve are restless and have been for nearly one and a quarter centuries.

One spirit in particular roams the library to this day. It is believed to be the shade of Henry Snowden, who died at the tender age of 15 months. He was swaddled in a burial gown, placed in a casket, and buried under the headstone that bears his name. His body was reclaimed by his parents as construction proceeded. He was reburied at the Allegheny Cemetery, so he should rest serenely. But the headstone that marked the place of his grave for 52 years resides in the library, where it is sometimes put on display as a rather macabre artifact of the library's origin. Young Henry seems to have an affection for that stone, since he continues to toddle along the hallways of the building containing it.

The head librarian here pooh-poohs any idea of hauntings at her library. She claims never to have seen any spirits there. She attributes all the various moans, groans, and unearthly cries to the settling of an ancient building with an antique plumbing and heating system.

Even so, wouldn't it be a simple solution to return the headstone to its owner at Section 16, Lot 145, Grave 1 in Allegheny Cemetery a few blocks away on Butler Street? Then at least one of the souls of the Lawrenceville Burying Grounds could find peace.

Turn around and head uphill on Fisk Street to Penn Avenue. Turn left, and in short order we'll be at the huge conglomeration of the new Children's Hospital of Pittsburgh.

Children's Hospital of Pittsburgh

**Liberace's White-Robed Nun
of St. Francis Hospital
4401 Penn Avenue
Pittsburgh**

On the site of the sparkling-new Children's Hospital of Pittsburgh was once a full-service, medium-sized hospital by the name of St. Francis. It was begun in 1865 by three Franciscan Sisters from Buffalo, New York as a 15-bed hospital. Over the next 137 years it grew into the St. Francis Health System encompassing three hospitals: one in Cranberry, one in New Castle, and the main one in Lawrenceville, all in Western Pennsylvania.

St. Francis was a teaching hospital with the Student Nurses' living quarters across 45th Street from the main hospital for many years and was forever dedicated to the treatment of all comers, regardless of ability to pay, to heal patients in, "body, mind, and spirit." Nobody needed to fear bankruptcy as a result of receiving treatment at St. Francis. It maintained this philosophy until the end, ignoring modern medicine's preoccupation with profit and over-compensation of executives. The end came in 2002 when finances forced it to close its doors. Pittsburgh's medical behemoth, University of Pittsburgh Medical Center(UPMC) came to the rescue, closed it for a few years, built a state-of-the-art medical complex, and reopened it as Children's Hospital of Pittsburgh in 2009.

This story takes place before all that happened. The date was November 23, 1963. It was little more than 24 hours since the 35th President of the United States, John Fitzgerald Kennedy had been assassinated in Dealey Plaza, Dallas, Texas. The Godfather of Bling, flamboyant entertainer and consummate pianist Wladziu Valentino Liberace, known to his countless fans simply as "Liberace" assumed that his evening show at the Holiday House in Monroeville, just east of Pittsburgh, would be canceled that evening. He thought that people would be in no mood for hilarity at this time of national mourning.

He spent his afternoon cleaning one of his many over-the-top costumes. The cleaning fluid he used had as its chief ingredient carbon tetrachloride, a dangerous liquid whose volatiles quickly enter surrounding air, replacing oxygen with its organ-damaging fumes. Not only did he do this in an unventilated room, he also took a couple of naps in that same room during that time.

As evening approached, he was informed by Holiday House management that his show would go on as scheduled. They told him his show was needed to lift a small bit of the pall hanging over people at that time and give them some respite from the pervading gloom.

He went on stage for his first evening performance but never completed the show. Part way through he collapsed on stage and was rushed through the eastern suburbs of Pittsburgh to St. Francis Hospital, the banshee wail of the ambulance clearing the way. The fumes from the cleaning fluid caused massive kidney failure.

A stroke of incredible luck was bestowed upon him. St. Francis Hospital had recently acquired a brand-new dialysis machine, one of the first in the area, if not the entire state. In spite of having this newest marvel of modern medicine at their disposal, while attaching his earthly body to the machine, the attending doctors told him that it would be a good idea for him to make whatever peace with God that he thought necessary. They estimated his chance of survival as 20 percent.

During the night that he thought was going to be his last, many things competed for prominence in his mind. But the one thing that he remembered more than all the others was a nun who came to his bedside and urged him to pray to Saint Anthony to intercede on his behalf with God. Liberace did as she suggested and enjoyed a remarkable recovery.

On his recovery, Liberace recounted his experience with doctors and other staff at the hospital who told him that there were no nuns who wore white habits at St. Francis Hospital. All of the nuns at that hospital were of the Franciscan order and wore dark colored habits. Nevertheless, Liberace credited his recovery to the hospital *and* the sister who wore the white habit. From that day on he devoted a part of his attention to the continuance of the hospital, conducted many fund raising events, donated large amounts of his personal wealth, and even had a lobby named in his honor. Whenever he was scheduled to perform in or near Pittsburgh, Liberace always made sure that the sisters of the hospital were provided with tickets.

Sadly, Liberace passed away on February 4, 1987 while his beloved hospital lingered, wasting away on the rack of economics for another 15 years. Hopefully, his benevolent, saintly Sister in White will stay on to care for the many, many sick and injured children who will enter through the doors of the new hospital built on that site.

A mile and a half further east on Penn Avenue brings us to the Pittsburgh house of Henry Clay Frick, one of the world's richest men of his time. He was also possibly one of the world's most tragic men of his time. Let's stop and examine his mansion, called Clayton.

Clayton

The Frick Art and Historical Center

7227 Reynolds Street
Pittsburgh

Henry Clay Frick is a study in contrasts. He was the consummate capitalist, embodying all that word connotates, both positive and negative. He was one of the foremost of the Robber-Barons of the industrial age, along with his one-time friend and partner, Andrew Carnegie. He was blamed for the infamous Homestead Massacre of July 6, 1892. That battle at the Homestead Works of Carnegie Steel that morning between striking steel workers and the Pinkerton goons hired by Frick left

16 men dead. Their blood stained the banks of the Monongahela River while Andrew Carnegie vacationed in Scotland, leaving Frick to take the heat. Troops had to be called out to quell the riots that resulted from his heavy-handed way of trying to stifle the strike. He spent the rest of his life with the weight of those sixteen deaths hung about his shoulders like the fabled albatross.

He was born at his grandfather's place, called West Overton, just outside of Scottdale, PA. As he grew to manhood, he learned the principle of, "vertical integration," from his grandfather, Abraham Overholt, who operated a distillery. Vertical integration is a manufacturing principle whereby the manufacturer controls all aspects of the manufacturing process from raw materials to finished product. Frick saw how this could be applied to the Steel Industry. By the time he was 30 years of age he was a multimillionaire at a time when that actually meant something. He partnered with Andrew Carnegie at the age of 32, and together they owned the largest producer of steel in the entire world, Carnegie Steel. These two were just about the richest men in the world at the time.

He left a slew of ghosts in his wake. West Overton, where he spent his early years, is one of the most haunted places in Westmoreland County. The home of Old Overholt and Pennsylvania Rye whiskeys is actually a cluster of buildings. It includes the distillery building, the Overholt Mansion and about a dozen other structures in various states of restoration. The buildings and grounds are haunted by mischievous entities that like to turn lights on and off, knock hats from heads, cameras out of hands, and rattle chains and implements in the barns. Clyde Overholt who committed suicide with a shotgun makes his appearance in one of the upper story windows of the mansion. And, another of the Overholt clan was found hanging from one of the trees on the grounds and makes his appearance in that manner to this day. The lady in blue wanders the grounds and sounds of people are heard in the coke ovens, even when the area is deserted.

Henry Clay Frick was the founder of the Southfork Fishing and Hunting Club. The failure of the club's earthen dam on May 31, 1889 resulted in the utter devastation of the city of Johnstown, PA along with a tremendous loss of life. This single event is responsible for dozens of hauntings in the Johnstown-St. Michaels area along the path of the Little Connemaugh River.

Small wonder then, that Clayton, where he made a home for himself and his family is so haunted that the ghosts have to jostle one another for room. Although the building's address is listed as Reynolds Avenue, the great dowager overlooks Penn Avenue which is the western end of the Penn-Lincoln Highway. This part of Penn Avenue was shared by the original U.S. Routes 22 and 30, as well as Pennsylvania Route 8 through eastern Pittsburgh and the eastern suburbs for a ways.

Martha Frick was the absolute light of Henry's life. Maybe it was the contrast between her childhood innocence and the everyday dirty dealings of his life that gave him a safe haven from the hatred that he had to endure. She was the second of his four children and he adored her, doted on her and gave her everything that one of the richest men in the world could give.

One week before her sixth birthday in early August, 1891, she died as a result of ingesting a pin and the infection that it brought. Maybe it was her wish to continue to bring a bit of happiness to this mansion that has seen so much tragedy that keeps her coming back. She flits through the vegetation surrounding the mansion, apparently playing a game of tag.

The following year, 1892, in the midst of the Homestead Steel Strike, Henry Clay Frick, Jr. was born. The family hoped that his birth would help to alleviate some of the pain and suffering that hovered over the family. It was not to be so. Henry's namesake died in his infancy leaving the family, once again heartbroken.

One of the things that Henry Clay Frick built for his children was a full-sized fabulous playhouse right on the grounds of the mansion. It was so opulent that it even included a bowling alley on the first floor. Though it was built some years after her death, Martha Frick enjoys its amenities, since the sounds of children are often heard squealing with delight when no one is there.

In the expanded Carriage House is the collection of Frick automobiles and carriages. Tour followers aren't the only ones to visit here. Apparitions in the period dress of the late 1800s and early 1900s are also seen wandering the exhibition, no doubtably approving of the millionaire's taste in transportation.

Adelaide Howard Childs Frick, Henry's wife and the mother of this star-crossed, some say cursed, family never got over the death of her young children. She left this mortal coil in 1931, but stays on at Clayton. She is seen walking about the mansion checking to make sure that everything is clean, neat, and in its right place. She still oversees the staff much as she did when alive.

In the parlor of the mansion otherworldly reflections of the children's funerals appear with Adelaide Frick in attendance.

>*<

The original Route 22 proceeds along Penn Avenue through the eastern suburbs of Wilkinsburg, Wilkins, and Churchill on its way to our next stop in the suburb of Monroeville. Penn Avenue, which carried Route 22 veers off to the left at a traffic signal two blocks after Swissvale Ave.

Since there is nothing but residential areas along that way, I recommend staying to the right onto Ardmore Blvd., then following the signs to Interstate 376 East which is also the new path of U.S. 22. Once we're on Route 376, we'll take the Business Route 22 Exit to Monroeville. Our next stop is on the hill behind Monroeville Mall.

If, instead of taking the first exit to the mall, we continue on to the next traffic signal, you will notice a car dealership and a Toys R Us on the left hand side of the road. They are in the approximate location of the Old Holiday House, the night club where Liberace collapsed prior to his fateful meeting with the "Sister in White."

Right now, we are taking a short detour. Set your GPS for Patton Street Extension in Monroeville, PA and we'll go to Restland Cemetery.

Roaming Rosie

Old Restland Cemetery
Patton Street Extension
Monroeville

Off to the side of Route 22 in Monroeville, up over the hill behind Monroeville Mall, lies the home of Roaming Rosie, Restland Cemetery.

Don't confuse Roaming Rosie with Walking Rosie. They are two different entities entirely.

Walking Rosie is a stone monument in the shape of a walking person. Shining a flashlight on it after dark creates an illusion of motion and makes the figure on the monument appear to be walking. There are even supposed to be pictures of this phenomenon, although I have never seen one. But rest easy – it's just an optical illusion.

Not so Roaming Rosie. She slowly walks the lightly treed rolling meadow of Restland Cemetery at night, knife in hand, looking for her ex-lover.

Roaming Rosie is a victim in many ways. Some say she was a victim of unrequited love, jilted by her lover and left with a broken heart. Those who have seen her slowly walking the grounds in the pastoral quietude of Restland Cemetery know that even her eternal rest was taken from her. The final indignity was the removal of her monument.

Over the years countless visitors who have come to this place to pay respects to their loved ones have seen this young lady in early 20th-century attire.

She is a mystery. Nobody knows the true story of Rosie. Nobody knows when she died or even her full name. Her monument simply said "Rosie," and now even it has disappeared. The monument had been splashed with a red liquid assumed to be blood, and it was found knocked over more than once. Speculation has it that cemetery officials had it removed because they thought it was attracting teenagers and vandals who were "investigating" the legend.

Rosie isn't the only ghost at Restland. The smell of gunpowder pervades the area around a veteran's grave. A girl of 8 or 10, wearing clothing popular with pioneers, flits among the trees. Shades of people long gone sit near their graves to greet visitors.

In light of all this ethereal activity, maybe it's time for a name change. Perhaps it should be called "Restless Cemetery."

>*<

From here, let's continue east on Route 22 through Monroeville and over the hill a few miles away to the Monroeville-Murrysville border, the home of the hamburger-loving ghost.

Wendy's Restaurant

5076 William Penn Highway
Monroeville

It's definitely not Dave Thomas, the founder of the Wendy's fast-food restaurant chain, hanging around to get a double cheeseburger and fries, or even a rich, thick Frosty. Dave has gone on to his heavenly reward and seems satisfied to stay there after a busy life of nonstop work.

It must be someone else from the other side who walks through the restaurant when it isn't quite open for business. When he is approached, he turns a corner and disappears. Employees are treated to spectral conversations in the dining area when it is devoid of customers, and the hanging lamps there swing to and fro with no earthly assistance. Then an unseen hand suddenly quells the swinging of the lamp. Patrons as well as employees have walked into spots that are unexplainably cold.

It turns out that this particular spot is directly over an old coal mine that witnessed the deaths of several miners. Their spirits get the blame for these unusual happenings. Maybe they tired of the mundane contents of their lunch buckets and want something different. After all, decades of the same midday meal can get tiresome. Or is the ground settling into the mine? That might explain the unsteady lamps, but it doesn't explain the apparition.

Instead of asking, "Do you want fries with that?" the employees could offer you a spectral dining companion if you don't want to eat alone.

After we wash down that burger and fries, let's get back on the road heading east. We may just meet a rather less benign shade seven miles east on this William Penn Highway near Export, PA.

Lessig Cemetery Ghosts
By
Maxine Ruble

Mark Drive
Export

Let's let Maxine Ruble tell us the tale of the haunted, abandoned cemetery on the hill north of U.S. 22 right before its intersection with PA Route 66. Its occupants are less than happy being left in the soil to be forgotten. But, when someone visits, they are not quite hospitable.

In a rural corner of western Westmoreland County sits the old Lessig Cemetery. It is situated on a very old road which was a main route for farmers in the area to drive their livestock to market. I have lived across from this cemetery all my life and played in it as a child when it was an overgrown wooded area with grapevines hanging from the oak trees. Legend has it there are Native Americans buried there though I doubt it. The first recorded burial was Patrick McKinney who was noted as "the town drunk" and was buried there in 1805, though the cemetery had already been in use by this time with prior internments. There are veterans buried from the Revolutionary War and War of 1812. It's estimated there are about twenty five graves, but I do not know if this includes the ones that were marked only with field stones or unmarked altogether. The last burial seems to have been in 1871 but there is an account of a later burial in the early 1900's. My particular favorite is the obelisk marked grave of John Van Dyke Stout, a War of 1812 veteran. I used to sit for hours on a fallen tree by his grave and "talk" with him when I was little and had no one else to play with. There are also a number of children's graves that always made me feel so sad.

By the time my children were growing up in the 70's, a neighbor had cleared the cemetery and it was recognizable as such instead of just a patch of "woods". It was during this time that both my son and daughter were "visited" in their rooms at night. My daughter was "visited" by a little girl who was dressed, according to my daughter's description, in what would have been appropriate for the mid 1800's. The little girl was crying and when my daughter asked why, she said "Because no one believes anymore," and then she vanished. Needless to say, my daughter was quite frightened. But since she was only about ten years old we passed the occurrence off as "imagination". My son had a frequent visitor of a tall thin man dressed in black with a tall hat. This apparition never spoke and would appear in my son's room or at night in the yard. My daughter also saw it one day in broad daylight in our living room. Both my son and daughter described this apparition as looking like a black paper silhouette of a man that could move and would suddenly just vanish. These appearances lasted over a period of about ten years. When my son was young, we passed these off as "imagination" as well, but I began to wonder when the appearances continued into his teen years. It was also during this time that a visitor saw the shadow of a man appear before her in the bathroom. She was a person we barely knew who had never been to the house before and had not heard any of our stories.

She came and whispered to me, "Do you have a ghost?" Rather than answer her, I asked her why she asked. She related her experience to me. For a while we were bothered with the lights being turned off and on in the bathroom and with the toilet suddenly flushing by itself. Perhaps the ghost was drawn to the bathroom because he had never seen anything comparable during his lifetime.

It wasn't until about 2005 that a mutual friend, R.E. who was interested in history and hauntings, asked my son and me to take him and a friend of his, E.S. through the cemetery at night while E.S. operated a tape recorder and R.E. took pictures. My son and I were not pleased about this but agreed, though we refused to venture into the far right corner where there was a grave separated somewhat from the others and where the temperature was always lower than the surrounding area. It was quite dark as we stumbled through the cemetery. We did not hear anything and I did not see anything though R.E. thought he saw a shadow moving in his peripheral vision. R.E. spoke out, asking any spirits to show themselves, but nothing happened. Finally we gave up and returned to my house across the road. Though we had heard nothing, E.S. wanted to play his tape. We sat and listened to the few recorded words spoken intermittently by someone in our group and mostly static.

Suddenly, a very gravelly voice, whispery but clearly audible, said, "Get out!" We looked at one another in stunned surprise and asked, "Did you hear that?" E. S. played the tape over and we heard the same voice. If you could have heard it, it would have given you chills as it did us. When E. S. played the tape the next day at his house, the voice was not there. Needless to say, neither my son nor I have any desire to lead anyone else through the cemetery at night for any reason, so don't even ask.

Heading east on Route 22 again, keep a sharp eye out on the shoulder of the road and maybe you'll see what a friend of mine saw on her way just east of New Alexandria some months back. Read on ...

Time Travel Civil War Soldier Of Route 22 New Alexandria
by
Marge Burke

In 1793 Arthur Denniston ran a saw mill on the bank of the Loyalhanna Creek where the path from Hanna's Town crossed it. That year he advertised lots for sale to build a town on the hill overlooking that creek. The town was to be called "New Town of Alexandria." Today, it's called New Alexandria on the map and New Alex by its citizens. At one time, Route 22 went right through the middle of this rural setting on Main Street. Years ago, in deference to the traveling public's desire to whiz right on by anything interesting, the powers that be decided to bypass the town with a four lane highway.

You don't have to ride that four lane and it is less than a five minute detour to cruise slowly through this beautiful microcosm of rural America on its tree-lined streets. Just turn onto Main Street off Route 22 a bit after the intersection with U.S. Route 119. Its population in 2000 was less than 600, so you can see that it hasn't yet succumbed to urban sprawl.

Just East of town was the New Alexandria Airport, a small strip that never grew to a commercial success. But it has been reincarnated as Pittsburgh Raceway Park, a nationally-famous drag strip that attracts competitors and spectators from all over. If you get there on Test and Tune Day, you can run the drag strip in your own car. Who knows, your family flivver just may be a fire-breathing monster in disguise.

Perhaps because of its natural beauty combined with the friendliness of its neighborly citizens, people who are born in New Alex tend to stay here. People who, for one reason or another leave, tend to return.

150 years ago our country was engaged in a civil war that pitted state against state and sometimes even brother against brother. New Alex was no different from any of the other small towns throughout Westmoreland County when the call to arms was raised. She freely gave of her young men to preserve the Union.

When that war was over, those men who survived returned home. This is a story about one such man, who after 150 years is still trying to get back home to his beautiful New Alexandria. It is best told by the person who experienced it:

I saw him clear as day along side the road. And I knew immediately who he was.

It was a comfortable August evening, with the sun just beginning to move behind the tree line but still bright. A breeze cooled the air despite the bright sun. There was very little traffic, and the construction was over for the day. Both lanes were in the south bound lanes but there were no delays. I was thinking how lovely the sky was with the deep blue heavens and the huge fluffy white clouds hanging like puffs of cotton.

The man was walking along the berm of the road facing traffic. He took his time, leaning a bit on the iron rod he had in his right hand. The first thing I noticed was his hat. It was dark blue, round and squat, with a small flat visor across the forehead. He wore dark blue trousers, thick and belted, with wide suspenders arching over his shoulders. His shirt was gray, short sleeved and lighter weight.

I couldn't see his whole boot, but I could see they were black and had rounded toes. There was a leather pouch on a strap slung over his head and draped from his left shoulder to his right hip. He had a fuzzy, dark beard that filled his face and chin.

I slowed as much as I could; there were no cars behind me but a number coming towards me. The man stopped his trek and leaned against a road sign, staring out over the highway as if he'd never seen one before. And in that moment I knew. There was only one explanation. This man was caught in a time travel snare. And the iron rod was a long barreled rifle with a bayonet on the end.

He was a misplaced soldier from the Civil War.

You can argue with me that it was just a scruffy man with a stick, trying to determine how much longer the road would be torn up. Or you can say that the sun was playing tricks on my vision. Maybe.

But if you had been driving east on Routes 22/119 between Blairsville and New Alexander that day, you would have seen him too. And you would be just as convinced as I am that this soldier slipped through a crack in the universe somewhere and ended up standing in front of me, watching the cars drive past as if they were the miracles that they are.

I want to believe in my soldier. I do believe in my soldier. I just hope that whoever he is, and wherever he came from, he can find his way home or make his home here, and tell everyone who would listen about the day he fell into the 21st century from 1861.

Because I saw him, clear as day. And I knew.
Marge Burke.

Four and a half miles east of New Alexandria we will come to the intersection of PA Route 982 on our right. Don't go that way, It'll take you to Derry and that's not part of our trip. Instead, turn left onto Livermore Road, if you are so inclined. This road, which eventually peters out, turns into a dirt road, and eventually terminates in an unpaved parking lot and trail head for the West Penn Rail to Trails bicycle and hiking trail. If I were you, I wouldn't waste my time. All that is to be seen of the town of Livermore is the surface of the Conemaugh River and a visit to the cemetery will only get you arrested for trespassing.

Instead, stop five miles further along on Route 22 at Dean's Diner, enjoy lunch at one of Pennsylvania's final remaining classic diners, and visit Livermore virtually in the following story.

Livermore, PA and Livermore Cemetery

Livermore was an unfortunate town. It was founded in 1827 by John Livermore, who courted immortality by naming the town after himself. He located the town on the bank of the Conemaugh River alongside the Pennsylvania Canal Main Line Western Division, which served Pittsburgh and Johnstown, along with points in between. The Pennsylvania Railroad followed a couple of decades later, and a station was located in Livermore. The combination of canal, railroad, and roadways made Livermore a commercial crossroads. But for some reason, the town never grew to its full potential. Its largest population spikes were in 1870 and 1890, when it boasted 211 residents.

Perhaps that was because the town was built on the banks of the flood-prone Conemaugh River before the days of effective flood control. Minor to moderate flooding was an annual event during the spring snow melt from the mountains upstream, and disastrous floods occurred in 1889 and 1936. The 1889 flood so damaged the entire Juniata Branch of the Pennsylvania Canal that commercial freight from points east of Johnstown no longer came through, leading to the demise of the canal system and the little towns along its path. In fact, the 1940 census reported only 113 residents, and half of those moved away in the next ten years, leaving only 57 behind to populate the little town by 1950.

The last nail in the coffin that sent the town to a watery grave was driven in 1952, when the Army Corps of Engineers flooded the town with the creation of the Conemaugh Dam downstream as part of the Flood Control Acts of 1936 and 1938. The last 57 residents were relocated and the town was razed before the waters rose. Although Livermore was sent to the depths of Conemaugh Lake, its sacrifice has saved untold dollars and lives throughout the lower Conemaugh, Kiskimenetas, Allegheny, and upper Ohio River Valleys.

There is another reason given for the town's demise. Legend tells of a witch who lived in Livermore during the 1800s. She was apprehended by the townsfolk whilst practicing her craft. The complexities of a trial were not afforded her, and the mob tied her to a handy pole and piled kindling about her feet. A torch was applied, the wood flamed, and she was perished on the spot – but not before she screamed a curse on the town and its people.

Since nobody offered any water to quench the flames of her execution, she condemned the town itself to perish by an excess of that liquid that was in such scant supply for her. Had I been there, I might have moved to higher ground. You know–just in case. And this is how the town got the nickname Satan's Seat. Supposedly the town was her throne and she was a minion of the devil. Now, after careful research and examination of public records from the town's establishment until the first great flood of 1889, I can find no credible account of the demise of a witch at the hands of the townspeople. Maybe it happened, maybe it didn't.

There are other stories about this luckless town. One is that, when the water is low after a long dry spell, you can see the tops of the buildings jutting from the water's surface. Well, not the real buildings. The Corps of Engineers razed every building to the ground before the waters from the dam backed up. But if you stand on the bank of the Conemaugh River Dam, overlooking the site of the long-gone town on a dewy spring or fall morning when the mist rises up from the water, you might see the ghosts of those buildings, just as I have. The town that witnessed so much destruction during its century-and-a-quarter rises from the mist as if to say, "I may be gone, but my spirit lives on." At least that's what I thought on that June morning a little after dawn when I saw a couple of chimneys and rooftops where none should be.

The railroad right of way is gone now, replaced by a rails-to-trails pathway called the West Penn Trail that runs 17 miles from Blairsville to Saltsburg. Walking or cycling the path in the vicinity of Livermore brings some people face to face with wandering apparitions who fade in and out of existence. These may be the shades of people who have had their rest disturbed while interred at the Livermore Cemetery.

This cemetery has become a sort of a cult destination. Some tote alcoholic libations in the hopes of meeting a ghost who is unhappy with being moved when the cemetery was relocated by the Corps of Engineers before they flooded the town. But it never happened. The cemetery has always been right where it is, on the bluff overlooking the Conemaugh Valley. The only spirits these visitors see are those fueled by the alcohol they bring with them. Others come to the cemetery in hopes of seeing a zombie. They think that George Romero's movie *Night of the Living Dead* was filmed there. Wrong! It was filmed at a cemetery in Evans City, an hour and a half ride to the west. Plus, it was a *movie*. What part of that don't they get?

While researching this book, I visited the cemetery and climbed down the hillside facing the river. The desecration that has taken place over the years is sickening. I found numerous tombstones that had been toppled from their rightful place and sent tumbling down the hill, many breaking into pieces. At the bottom of the hill, tombstone bases have been used as hearths for campfires. The abundance of empty beer cans gives mute evidence of the type of people who violating this hallowed ground. It is my fervent hope and prayer that the spirits of those who have been disturbed by these criminals track down the people responsible for this desecration and make them pay. If they fail, I know that karma will prevail.

Please allow the citizens of this town, which has suffered so much, some repose in their afterlife.

>*<

Old Route 22 feeds into the town of Blairsville and becomes Market Street. We'll turn left onto Pennsylvania Route 217 and head a couple of miles south to our next destination.

Torrance State Mental Hospital

**121 Longview Drive
Derry, PA**

A little over a mile south of Blairsville along Route 217 you will find yourself crossing the Conemaugh River. At the top of the hill is a nondescript country lane called Torrance Road. Down that road, with beautiful rolling meadows on both sides and the Chestnut Ridge as a background, lies Torrance State Hospital, a place of unspeakable terrors for hundreds, maybe thousands of people.

Its original intention was an admirable one. It was to be a place of refuge for people whose mental frailties made it impossible for them to take care of themselves. The doors to the Torrance Insane Asylum opened in

1919, admitting five patients in that first year. Its patient population quickly exceeded the staff's ability to humanely treat patients. Instead, mentally ill patients, those called "retarded," people referred for behaving erratically, and those committed by the courts for antisocial behavior (and judged to be criminally insane) were all warehoused together. Before the institution had celebrated its fiftieth anniversary, its patient population exceeded 3,000. This city of unfortunates was run by five doctors overseeing a staff that was supposed to be dedicated to the care, treatment, and welfare of their charges.

They tried. They really did. But they were doomed to failure. The hospital used what were cutting-edge medical treatments at the time, including both electro and insulin shock. Hydrotherapy was tried. Prefrontal lobotomies that reduced patients to vegetative states were popular for a while. What was euphemistically called chemotherapy consisted of keeping patients in a drugged state so they wouldn't be a bother to the staff. The theory seemed to be that a quiet patient is a progressing one..

Less palatable methods were also used. Some patients had to be restrained "for their own good." Restraining methods ranged from being placed in a straitjacket for hours on end to being wrapped in wet sheets from head to toe for an extended period to being strapped to a cot. A patient who was particularly unruly might find himself in chains, after being subjected to a rigorous beating. Beatings were part of the place's daily routine.

Rumors of the inhumane treatment of patients were discussed every day in the hamlet of Torrance on the banks of the river a scant half mile away. Workers from the hospital mentioned hangings, torture, and deaths. Patients were burned and suffocated, all in the name of treatment.

Patient-on-patient violence was common, and so were escapes.

Thankfully, this all came to an abrupt end in the 1960s when the deinstitutionalization movement took hold. New definitions of what constitutes mental disability were implemented. The Torrance Hospital for the Insane was found to be inhumane and unsafe for anybody, patients or staff. The buildings were closed and used only for storage until they were eventually found unfit for even that purpose. Most were torn down.

Today a state-of-the-art psychiatric medical facility has replaced the hospital of horror. The new hospital's mission is to treat patients, get them into a regimen of psychiatric and/or psychological care, and return them to their previous environments as functioning members of society.

But this all came with a price that was paid by previous residents. Maybe that's why so many of them have remained when their earthly husks have long since been buried and forgotten.

Patients who have passed on are frequently observed aimlessly walking in the wide meadows surrounding the facility. It's as though they have escaped but don't know where to go. When approached, they fade into nothingness.

You can reach the second floor of one of the old buildings only by climbing a dangerously deteriorated stairway. At the end of the hall is the only room with a door. It was once occupied by an elderly lady who rocked in her chair for hours on end. Although she is invisible now, she continues rocking into eternity, and the creaking of the rocker on the bare wood echoes throughout that floor.

Footsteps are heard treading on floors and steps where no one walks, and the sounds of doors opening and closing ring throughout buildings where the doors are long gone. Unexplained booms catch the attention of workers, visitors, and patients alike.

One haunt in particular roams the former morgue. She is thought to be a young girl who came to visit her mother only to find that her mother was dead, either from mistreatment or from murder. She runs the halls of the mortuary giggling and laughing, playing a game of hide and seek that she always wins because nobody can ever find her.

The doors on long-since deactivated elevators open and close at will, providing a lethal drop for the unwary.

If you decide to visit this place, observe from your car. If you leave it parked anywhere unattended, you may come back to find that your windshield wipers have been turned upside down by unseen hands. Besides, the grounds are restricted state property and heavily posted against trespassing. If you are caught roaming the grounds, you will be arrested.

Stay in your car, get back on Route 217, and head north back into Blairsville. As you cross the Conemaugh River entering Blairsville, take a look upstream. The river has just come through the Packsaddle Gap from the little town of Bolivar a few miles away. Read on to learn of Tom Skelton's ill-fated love of Maria McDowell.

~II~
THE ALLEGHENY MOUNTAINS

Birthplace of the nation's iron, coke, coal, and railroading industry.

THE FIRST OF THE MOUNTAINS
The Chestnut Ridge

The Repentant Lover of Packsaddle Gap

The Conemaugh River Through the Gap

Packsaddle Gap is a chasm cut through the Chestnut Ridge of the Allegheny Mountains by the Conemaugh River between the rural hamlet of Bolivar and the town of Blairsville. Studded with riffles and small rapids, it is been a perennial favorite of kayakers and canoeists looking for a pleasant afternoon on a scenic river. The rugged terrain of the 1,300-foot-deep gorge is unsuitable for home building. This fortunate prevention of human incursion makes it home to abundant wildlife, cherished by hunters and birdwatchers alike.

However, the path that follows the natural course of

the Conemaugh River didn't escape the notice of those entrepreneurs who had a stake in moving people and goods to and from the nation's westerly cities. After all, rivers were the nation's highways long before the car became ubiquitous. So the Gap became home to the Pennsylvania Canal (which was discussed in the story about the ill-fated town of Livermore). Likewise, the Pennsylvania Railroad hugged the river's shores, following the natural slope of the declivity, which saved the builders untold thousands, perhaps millions, of dollars.

It was the Gap's untamed wilderness that brought about its most tragic day.

A young Thomas Skelton and his bride-to-be, Maria McDowell, were out in the gorge for a day's hunting, not an unusual activity in the early to mid-1800s. Tom intended to bag a deer, perhaps as a gift for his future father-in-law. Maybe Maria, often lovingly called "New Moon" by Tom, had packed a picnic lunch in honor of the day. In all probability, they were dressed in everyday attire, he in broadcloth trousers and shirt of tan or brown, and she in a skirt or dress of similar material. If it was cool, they both likely wore jackets or vests made of animal hide. The reports don't really mention their clothing.

At some point, the pair became separated. It was no big thing. Voices carry well in the Gap, and a few shouts would be sufficient to reunite them. Or Tom's lovely New Moon would simply return to her parents' cabin on the ridge and he'd see her later.

While scouting the gorge, Tom noticed a flash of brown amidst the greenery of the brush. It was the right shade of brown for a deer. He shouldered his rifle, took aim, and fired. His target collapsed into the shrubbery and he raced to retrieve his prize, visions of sizzling venison steak dancing across his imagination.

Imagine his horror when he discovered, not the carcass of a freshly killed whitetail deer, but the lifeless body of his own Marie, his New Moon. She was shot dead on the spot, the victim of mistaken identity. Tom wasn't the first nor the last hunter in Pennsylvania to shoot and kill another human being he'd mistaken for game, but he was one of the very few to slay a loved one in such a manner. Now, instead of presenting venison for the dinner table, he was gently carrying home the only daughter of Donald McDowell, her life extinguished by the man who loved her.

Mr. McDowell and his frail, blind wife went about their daily routine within the confines of their cozy little house on the ridge, unaware of the devastating news that was approaching. Maybe they were preparing potatoes and greens to add to the hoped-for venison their daughter and her betrothed were hunting.

The day was waning, and Tom paused on the opposite river bank for a rest as a late day thunderstorm roared through the gap. He may even have been within seeing distance of his dreaded destination when the huge bolt of lightning struck the ridge just below the cabin. The cabin, as well as Mr. and Mrs. McDowell, rode the resultant landslide down the side of the gorge into the Conemaugh River and were washed away in the storm-fueled rushing waters, never to be recovered. Mercifully (if that is the proper word), they never learned of the demise of their one and only daughter.

Not so Tom. He spent the rest of his life living with his personal tragedy, becoming a hermit roaming the gap.

People met him from time to time as he aged and became another part of the folklore of the valley, but nobody ever knew what became of him. He just stopped wandering and people forgot about him. Until 1881, when Frank Cowan of Greensburg – an attorney, physician, writer, and one-time personal secretary to President Andrew Johnson – penned a story about Tom Skelton's afterlife activities.

As a Pennsylvania Railroad train loaded with passengers and freight passed through the Packsaddle Gap, a lone white man stepped onto the track. He rested the butt of his rifle on the ballast between the rails, crossed his arms and rested them on the barrel, and stared intently at the side of the mountainous gorge, as Cowan puts it, "through the gloom of the approaching night, and not see the approaching headlight until—-Horrible! Horrible! The old man is ground beneath the wheels."

The engineer immediately applied all the emergency braking power available to him. The massive line of cars and locomotive ponderously thundered to a halt and sat puffing and steaming. The crew ran back along the tracks to the site of the accident to find what was left of the victim. But they never found any trace of him. They had encountered the ghost of Tom Skelton, forever retracing his steps on that fateful day when he lost his love, the beautiful New Moon. Forever hoping to reverse that tragic turn of events.

Twice more train crews went through this fearsome experience. Frank Cowan continued his recollection, "Thrice already the train has stopped at this point; and thrice the engineer has descended from the train, and with a sickening heart walked back the ties in expectation of finding the mangled remains of an old man lying on the track–or in the declivitous side of the mountain along which the railroad has been cut–or a hundred feet below on the bank of the river where he might have landed.

"But the light of the lantern has not revealed to the engineer, nor the light of day to the laborer, the mangled body of Wild Tom Skelton, the weird old man that haunts the Packsaddle Gap."

That fateful lightning strike that caused the ground under the McDowell cabin to break away and fall into the gorge? It left behind a rock outcropping carved into the profile of a man's face. Tom Skelton himself commented that it bore a remarkable resemblance to his intended father-in-law, Donald McDowell.

The railroad employees weren't the only ones who encountered the ghost of Tom alongside the Conemaugh River in the gap. During the years when that part of the river was a link on the Pennsylvania Main Line Canal, the ghost of a ragged old man would appear on the towpath from time to time, sending the mules that pulled the canal boats into paroxysms of terror.

As the years went by, appearances by Tom's ghost became more and more infrequent – until about 20 years ago. As the gap has been rediscovered by various groups who enjoy the chance to be up close and personal with rugged nature, sightings of Old Tom have increased.

People floating along the river on a quiet late afternoon just about sundown have heard the plaintive call of the grief-stricken old man calling out with hope that he hasn't really shot and killed the love of his life. You too, can walk the bank of the river and hear him calling, "Maria, Maria," a sob caught in his throat for eternity.

Let's leave Tom to contemplate his mournful existence in solitude while we head east on Route 22 and meet up with a colonial horse thief. Pay attention to not only the road but the sides of the road while ascending the mountain just east of Blairsville. This area is the home of Chessie, the Chestnut Ridge's own Sasquatch (aka Bigfoot). Many motorists wind up needing the services of a towing company along this stretch of road because of an unfortunate meeting with a whitetail deer. So far, none has reported bending their car around a roaming Bigfoot – and you don't want to be the first.

Next we'll visit the town of Armagh, a couple of miles along.

Heading east on Route 22, the next right turn after Old Clay Pike is West Philadelphia Street, the main street that runs through Armagh, PA. It is also Route 22's original road and even had another name in the distant past: Old Stone Pike.

The Horse Thief of Armagh

**Old Clay Pike
Armagh**

Time was when a fellow by the name of John "Yank" Brown came to the little hamlet that had sprung up along that pike and saw the opportunity to conduct a little commerce. Armagh was ideally situated midway between Ebensburg and Blairsville for an overnight stop for travelers. John opened a tavern to wash the dust from the throats of those travelers. He must not have been a very astute businessman because he found the need to supplement his income by relieving people of their horses. Now, horses aren't the easiest thing to hide and it really isn't worthwhile to sell them one at a time. So,

John Brown stabled that stolen horseflesh in one of the many caves that dot the hillsides on the ridges surrounding Armagh.

When he had accumulated enough purloined ponies, he drove them to market under the cover of darkness where they were auctioned to unsuspecting bidders. John wasn't the brightest beacon of brilliance in the area but even he knew better than to show up around town with an unexplainable amount of fresh cash. John was well aware that missing horses, plus new-found money meant that his neck would meet a noose. So, he squirreled his money away, supposedly hiding it in another of the caves in the area. Some people say that his treasure is hidden under a rock, others say he buried it, and still others think he hid it in a hollowed log. Nevertheless, nobody has ever found it and its location has sunk into the murky waters of folklore.

Not so John and his horses. Park along the western end of what is now called Philadelphia Street on a quiet night during those hours best suited for smuggling stolen horses to market. Say, after 3AM and before 6 AM, those hours when anything can and usually does happen. Roll down the windows, turn off the radio, and listen. Just listen. If the approaching day is one that John "Yank" Brown feels is a good one to market his horses, you will hear the thundering of a dozen or so horses being driven along the pike in that direction. Don't bother to ask him about the treasure. You might be able to hear the horses, but you will see neither them nor John.

>*<

Feeling energetic? OK then, take the Route 403 exit off Route 22 and travel the mile and a half or so to Dilltown at the bottom of the hill. We can rent a bike at "Just Pedalin" right next to the aptly-named Ghost Town Trail there. Then we'll take a leisurely ride through a handful of ghost towns along the bike trail.

Ghostly Advice from the Lady in White

The Ghost Town Trail
Dilltown

What's the Ghost Town Trail? Simply put, it's 36 miles of nearly undiscovered beauty along the wooded banks of Black Lick Creek in Indiana and Cambria Counties. It follows the path of various railroads that served the abandoned towns that sprang up along the river to provide iron ore and coal to the voracious steel and iron industry in western Pennsylvania during the late 19th and early 20th centuries.

At least one resident of those mining towns has stayed on. Perhaps she feels that her advice just may save some other young lady from her fate. She is known for two things, her beauty and her white raiment. The Lady in White is most often seen roaming the area of the trail in the vicinity of Bracken, one of the Ghost Town Trail's abandoned villages. She also haunts Beulah Road in Nanty Glo, near one of the trail head parking lots.

Her purpose is twofold. She wanders the trail searching for the lover who murdered her. Woe be unto him when her search is successful. You know, "Hell hath no fury." And hoping that others can benefit from her gruesome ending, she visits the many parking areas along the trail that have become favorites of local couples seeking some solitude. She appears suddenly in their parked cars, either scaring the pants off the male or giving him incentive to put them back on. For the female, she offers her sweetest smile before fading from view. Her appearance is a warning that the relationship is going to turn abusive.

While absorbing the wooded scenery along the quietly swishing creek, there is no better place to make our headquarters than the Dillweed Bed & Breakfast, a turn-of-the-last-century home only a few feet from the trail.

Staying on the Ghost Town Trail, let's pedal along upstream until we get to Vintondale. If we aren't pedaling, we'll just ride in comfort in our car along the Black Lick.

A comprehensive website with links that give all the information about traveling the Ghost Town Trail is:

www.indianacountyparks.org/trails/gtt/gtt/html.

It has many links giving trail distances, amenities, and elevations.

The Haunt of the Eliza Furnace

**Ghost Town Trail
Vintondale, PA**

Just as you approach Vintondale along the Ghost Town Trail, the trail splits. A four-mile branch continues along to Rexis, then abruptly ends at U.S. Route 422. The main trail goes to the left through the town of Vintondale and continues on to Ebensburg, passing through Nanty Glo on its way. A hundred yards or so toward Vintondale from the split lies a large stone structure called the Eliza Furnace.

This furnace was in operation before the heyday of

coal mining along the Ghost Town Trail. The area had sufficient amounts of iron ore, lime, and timber for the manufacture of iron. Plus, it was ideally situated on the banks of a stream. So from 1846 to 1849 it provided up to 1,080 tons of pig iron a year. During peak operating times it employed 90 men and boys and 45 mules. Unfortunately, even at peak operating capacity, it wasn't financially feasible. Its fires were extinguished once and for all after only four years. It sits alongside the Ghost Town Trail as a perfect example of one of the last iron furnaces in the entire country that still sports its heat exchanger. Stop and read the historical markers that tell its tale.

Walk on up to the furnace and look inside. Look up the inside of the furnace to the top, where the heat exchangers are. Do you see the faint image of a pair of boots swinging gently in the dim recess? If so, you aren't the first. They belong to one of the original owners of the Eliza Furnace, David Ritter, who hanged himself there.

David Ritter and George Rodgers were business partners who saw the possibilities of building an iron furnace in this rural valley. All the ingredients for making the iron were nearby, and Pittsburgh, just 60 miles away, was a market for the pig iron.. Easy transport on the Pennsylvania Canal was just over the ridge at the Conemaugh River, less than 10 miles away. What could go wrong?

Everything. Messrs. Ritter and Rodgers must have faced financial ruin at the least, not to mention the wrath of those families that settled near the furnace and depending on it for their livelihood.

For David Ritter, the loss was even more personal. His son, while either working or playing around the furnace, fell in and was consumed by the flames. This, combined with his financial ruin, was enough for his wife to seek solace in the arms of his business partner. Shortly after the furnace closed, George Rodgers and Mrs. Ritter ran off together to start a new life elsewhere as far from the Eliza Furnace as they could get.

It was more than David Ritter could handle. He was in the depths of depression over the loss of his fortune, his son, and his wife. He climbed to the top of the furnace that symbolized his destruction and looped one end of a length of rope around a pipe of the heat exchanger and the other end around his neck. He then took a step into eternity.

Ever since that fateful day, his spirit has been wandering the area. Cyclists and walkers along the trail have seen him examining the furnace with a proprietary air, as though he was expecting the fires to be rekindled any minute.

Others, possibly including yourself, look up the stack of the furnace and see his boots at the bottom of his body swaying at the end of his makeshift hangman's rope.

On this mournful note, we'll get back onto the main road on Route 22 and head eastward to a mansion built for a queen—a queen of the stage.

Elmhurst Mansion

Cresson, PA

Imagine being the first number one super model in the world. Your face and body adorns everything from playing cards to magazine covers. Your name is known in every household in the country as the most beautiful woman in the world. You become a dancer in the chorus line of a Broadway show and are suddenly "discovered." Before you know it, you are in featured roles along the Great White Way and add the title of "Broadway Star" to your resume. You find yourself wooed by millionaires and international stars alike, from the fabled John Barrymore to ultra-rich New York Architect Stanford White. You are from the small industrial town of Tarentum, PA that has a population of 4,000. You are just 16 years old.

That's what Florence Evelyn Nesbit faced in 1901. After a lavish courtship, she was plied with champagne and lost her virginity to 47 year old Stanford White, called "Stanny," by his associates. He then passed her on to a friend of his, actor John Barrymore, who was 21 at the time. Smitten by her beauty and being an honorable man, he asked for her hand in marriage. Based on the advice of her mother who considered Mr. Barrymore's financial future as an actor to be uncertain, she turned him down.

Then she met Pittsburgh multimillionaire Henry Thaw and subsequently married him in 1905. Instead of an idyllic existence free from financial cares, she found herself a virtual prisoner in the Thaw Mansion, called Lyndhurst on Beechwood Boulevard in the Squirrel Hill section of the city.

Henry Thaw was obsessed with his wife's past showing symptoms of what today would be called paranoid schizophrenia fueled by a morphine addiction. On June 25, 1906, Henry Thaw and his young wife Evelyn attended a rooftop production of *Mam'zelle Champagne* at the Madison Square Garden. Also in attendance at a private table was Stanford White. During the closing production number, "I Could Love A Million Girls," Henry Thaw approached Stanford White. Standing less than three feet away, he shot White three times in the head, obliterating his face.

Standing over Stanford White's dead body waving his pistol in the air, Henry Thaw addressed the crowd, shouting, "He ruined my wife!"

What followed was a media frenzy and a courtroom sideshow that was called, "The Trial of the Century," the first of many given that appellation. Judged criminally insane, Henry Thaw was sentenced to an asylum in upstate New York. After seven years, his wealth managed to get him judged sane and he walked out a free man. He died in 1947 leaving his wife $10,000 of his

$1,000,000+ estate.

Evelyn finally passed on in 1967 after a career that never approached her earliest fame.

Now, during the brief early years of their marriage, Henry Thaw and Evelyn Nesbit-Thaw entertained guests at the Thaw summer mansion in Cresson, PA called Elmhurst. It was their getaway from the summer heat, smog, and soot of Pittsburgh until it was sold by the Thaw family in 1920. One room in particular is adorned with keepsake drawings of Evelyn when she was at her most beautiful. Even though she felt a prisoner in her marriage, she must have enjoyed her summers here, because she has returned here after her death.

Her spirit wanders the halls and rooms of the mansion, her visage sometimes appearing in mirrors. The financial instability of her early life and her life after the trial is evident in the way she husbands the electricity in the mansion, turning lights on and off at her whim.

Motorists have encountered her along Route 22 in the Cresson area in the guise of a young lady wearing a long white dress who tearfully asks to be taken to Elmhurst. She will get in the car and offer directions to the destination. Then, as they approach the gate to the mansion, she fades from sight and disappears.

Maybe she is trying to relive happier days when she didn't feel so much under the thumb of her husband and mother-in-law.

Her unhappy existence was depicted in the 1955 movie, "The Girl in the Red Velvet Swing," starring Joan Collins, Ray Milland, and Farley Granger.

Local, award-winning poet, Joan Grimes Kowalski has put pen to Evelyn's plight thusly:

Evelyn of Elmhurst
by
Joan Grimes Kowalski

Evelyn was a "Gibson Girl", a Broadway beauty queen,
Seduced by artist, Stanford White, when barely seventeen.

She went to Europe with Harry Thaw, a tour that changed her life
For he was strange, possessive, cruel – but she became his wife.

He built the Elmhurst Mansion to seclude his lovely bride
A hundred miles from Pittsburgh, far out in the countryside.

She had servants, jewels and luxuries she thought she'd never own
But never a guest, for in Harry's eyes, she was his and his alone.

With everything his wealth could buy, he thought she'd always stay
But Evelyn hated her "gilded cage", slipped out, and ran away.

Harry Followed her, mad with rage, trailed her both day and night
And found her, finally, in New York, dining with Stanford White.

Evelyn cringed from his anger but, "I'll save you!" was all he said

He drew his gun, three shots rang out, and Stanford White lay dead.

Harry Thaw was judged insane, not punished for his crime

And Evelyn dropped out of sight, forgotten for a time.

It wasn't till after Evelyn died, out in New York somewhere

That the shade of a lovely Gibson Girl appeared on the Elmhurst stair.

Sometimes, when no one's looking, she'll turn on the gas or light

And sometimes, she cries broken hearted sobs in the still of the Elmhurst night.

They say that she wants to destroy the house, but whether that's right or wrong

Her room stands just as she left it there, and nobody lives there long.

Could this be Evelyn's punishment for being a faithless wife?

To haunt forever the lonely house she hated so much in life.

And OK, OK, I know that the poem doesn't exactly dovetail with the actual facts of the case, but it tells the tale nicely. Besides, it's called *poetic license.*

Over on the other side of the new four-lane expressway lies a National Historic Site devoted to the Allegheny Portage Railroad. Let's go soak in some history and, while we're at it, visit a few denizens of the heyday of the railroad who have decided to linger on instead of crossing over.

The Lemon House at The Allegheny Portage Railroad Historic Site

Gallitzin, PA

During the early 1800s, Pennsylvania faced a dilemma. All the raw materials were in the western end of the state while the manufacturing facilities were in the eastern end of the state. An ingenious solution was found: The Pennsylvania Canal System. It however, faced a unique problem: the Allegheny Mountains. How to get the canal over those mountains?

To portage a vessel simply means to transport it overland between bodies of water. The problem to be solved was how to portage over the mountains between the Hollidaysburg Canal Basin and the basin at Johnstown that feeds into the canal system with the Pittsburgh terminus. Ever resourceful Pennsylvanians came up with the idea of combining a portage with a railroad and thus, the 36 mile Allegheny Portage Railroad was born in 1834. The fair weather only, 23 day trip between Philadelphia and Pittsburgh was shortened to 4 days. What followed was a flood of commerce both east and west that opened the western frontier and turned Pennsylvania into the industrial giant that it became.

Cargo and passengers were transported across the state in barges that were horse-drawn until reaching Hollidaysburg, then floated onto flat railroad cars and pulled uphill by small steam engines on the lesser inclines. On the steeper inclines they were attached to an endless rope and pulley system powered by stationary steam engines and winched up the slopes.

At the apex stands the historic and authentically restored Lemon House, a strategically located Restaurant and Tavern where travelers and workmen on the portage railroad could sup and sip during a brief break on their journey. During the 20 years of the railroads existence, Sam and Jean Lemon held a monopoly on providing food and drink for these people.

Passing through the doors of the Lemon House were thousands of people of all walks of life, including Ulysses S. Grant, Jenny Lind, and Charles Dickens. And, as happens with any great pioneering engineering accomplishment, there were accidents. The huge hemp ropes originally used to hoist the barges would, from time-to-time, snap with disastrous results. Men died. Railroad and construction accidents led to the demise of many more. The rigors of mid-19th century travel caught up with some of the less robust customers of the Lemon House and people expired within its walls.

National Park employees report that some of these unfortunates have stayed on for some reason or another. Maybe the camaraderie of the Inn was, and is, preferred over their intended destination or even the life that they had been living. They make their presence known with loud banging noises that have no earthly origin. Doors and windows open of their own volition at times, assisted by an otherworldly force, especially when the fog rolls in that is ubiquitous on the mountain top when the clouds are lowering.

Even the casual visitor to the Lemon House can feel the presence of its boisterous early inhabitants while standing in the barroom and catch a whiff of vegetable stew on the zephyrs that waft through from the dining room.

Take the next eastward exit on Route 22 and follow the signs into Gallitzin. Tour the Railroad Museum in town and take some time to see how the railroaders lived in the wonderfully restored caboose on the grounds. There is no admission fee. Adjacent to the museum are the famous Gallitzin Tunnels. On the other side of the tunnels is the site of the infamous Bennington Curve railroad disaster of 1947. That's our next story.

Ghosts of The Bennington Curve Disaster

**Sugar Run
Blair County**

Nothing remains of the town of Bennington except a small serene spot in the woods that holds the buried bodies of some of its former citizens. And this quiet little spot isn't affected by the disaster that happened on February 18, 1947. Its denizens rest securely, undisturbed in their graves.

But, I'm getting ahead of myself. Let's return to that blisteringly cold February morning a little after that coldest hour of the night, 3 AM.

The Pennsylvania Railroad's premier passenger express between Detroit and New York, The Red Arrow, sped through the Gallitzin Tunnel heading eastward nearly one and one-half hours behind schedule. The night was frigid, visibility was compromised by fog, the steam engines providing power had no speedometers, and the engineer was later found to be "virtually blind" in one eye due to cataracts.

The 238 passengers had settled for the night, lulled to sleep by the clickety-clack of the wheels on the rails and the gentle swaying of the cars. The other 40 riders were workers. Some concerned with the efficient operation of the train, others were postal employees, counting and sorting mail to be off loaded in Philadelphia and New York. Everything seemed to be as it should be, nothing was out of the ordinary.

At 3:25 AM, entering the Bennington Curve a bit beyond the tunnel, the Red Arrow derailed without warning and catapulted 5 of 14 cars, including its 2 locomotives down a 200 foot ravine, while 6 additional cars lie in a pile of twisted wreckage on the railroad right-of-way. A massive search and rescue operation was immediately set into motion.

When the final roll call of passengers and crew had been completed, 140 people had been rushed to area hospitals, overpowering their emergency rooms. 24 people didn't make it, they lost their lives on that snowy embankment.

But their spirits remain. If you park after dark by the Gallitzin Tunnels roll your windows down. Flash your headlights three times and turn the ignition off. As your car cools down, you may find yourself among the fortunate ones who hear animated conversation coming from the tunnel, growing nearer and nearer, culminating with the appearance of shadow figures at the tunnel's portal. Their conversations cannot be deciphered, but it doesn't sound as though those engaged in it are in any way aware of their disastrous end on the steel rails.

Another local legend that seems a bit apocryphal, since I have never been able to locate an actual witness, says that the wreck of the Red Arrow has a ghostly reenactment on the anniversary of the accident. Possibly those who have witnessed this reenactment are less than eager to share it beyond a close circle of friends because, in order to reach the accident site, criminal trespass on clearly-posted property is necessary.

Leaving Gallitzin, turn left on Tunnelhill Street and follow it. Watch for the sign that shows the way to the Horseshoe Curve. Or you can look for Lynch Road because that'll take us to the engineering triumph that effectively put the Portage Railroad out of business once and for all.

Haunted Horseshoe Curve

Altoona, PA

In 1854, the Pennsylvania Railroad completed the world-famous Horseshoe Curve ascending the Allegheny Mountains just west of Altoona. It was yet another engineering feat that pioneering Pennsylvanians accomplished to overcome what seemed to be insurmountable obstacles.

450 Irish immigrants, using only picks, shovels, and horse drags, filled in one deep ravine and built the incline on the side of the mountain in just over three years. This route newly designed by J. Edgar Thompson, chief engineer of the Pennsylvania Railroad, coupled with

more powerful locomotives, cut the travel time between Pittsburgh and Philadelphia from four days to 15 hours. When the first train chugged around the curve on February 15, 1854, it heralded the demise of the Allegheny Portage Railroad.

The construction workers who built the curve were a rough and tumble lot. They had to be to survive the long days of demanding physical labor in weather that ranged from blistering July afternoons to bone-chilling wintry days. No wonder that they liked to let off some steam when they got the opportunity.

One of those brawny men who carved the railroad line from the rock of the mountain looked upon those harsh conditions as his salvation. He and the love of his life had traveled the 4,500 miles from Ireland to Altoona to seek their fortune in the Promised Land of the United States. What money they could set aside from his meager earnings was going to build a home for the two of them and their future family. Maybe they planned to settle in Bennington, a few miles west of where they were building the famous curve. Nobody knows for sure.

One day, after spending sunup to sundown swinging a pick and loading rock onto horse-drawn wagons, the man stopped at one of the bars that had sprouted up to serve the workers. He, wanted to wash the dust and grit from his throat on his way home to his love. For some reason or another that would probably seem trite to us today, his manhood was challenged and he found himself at the center of a barroom brawl. In all likelihood it wasn't his first, but it was his last. He lost his life in that brawl, just one of many men who perished that way during those times. It was of no consequence, his name wasn't even mentioned in the *Altoona Tribune*.

But it was of great consequence to the love of his life. She pined away, unable to handle this tragedy, refusing to believe that his young life could be snuffed out so callously and quickly. Something inside her snapped and she waited day after day, expecting him to return home at the end of his shift. Of course he never did. But she never stopped waiting for him, even into the afterlife.

Many people have encountered the grief-stricken woman looking for her lover at the curve. She is found in the vicinity of the stone arched tunnel on the roadway beside the curve. Sometimes she'll appear walking through the portal of the tunnel; sometimes she is seen sitting on the stone wall right outside the tunnel or in the copse of spruce trees nearby. She dresses all in white and stands patiently waiting for the lover that will never come.

A number of legends have grown up about her and how to encounter her—for example, enter the tunnel at seven minutes before the hour of midnight during the night of the full moon, then flash your headlights three times and beep your car horn three times before driving the length of the short tunnel. But I don't think the spirit of the poor young lass cares about us, the time of night, the moon's cycle, or any light and sound code. She isn't waiting for us, she is waiting for her lost love.

Let's leave her to her fruitless quest and head downhill into the City of Altoona. The road in front of the Horseshoe Curve doesn't know what it wants to be called. As it passes the Horseshoe Curve, it is named Glenwhite Rd. after Glenwhite Run, the little rivulet that

it parallels. Then it picks up the name Veterans Memorial Highway. But it is also called Burgoon Rd. along this stretch. Then it becomes Kittanning Point Road as well. Luckily, we suffer this schizophrenia for less than a mile before making a right turn onto 58th Street.

This will take us down to where we make a left onto Route 764, also called West 6th Avenue. Watch for Route 36. That'll feed us onto 18th Street, which will become Buckhorn Road, another location of marriage plans gone awry, resulting in death, unrequited love – and of course, a ghost.

The Ghost of Buckhorn Mountain
Altoona, PA

Overlooking Interstate 99, just a few miles north of Route 22 lies Buckhorn Mountain. Legend has it that many years ago, a young man lost his life enroute to his wedding and his fiance froze to death searching for him on that fateful day. And she still searches the mountain for him to this day.

Joan Grimes Kowalski has immortalized her in an award-winning poem which she has given me permission to reprint here:

The White Lady of the Buckhorn
by
Joan Grimes Kowalski

If you drive the lonely Buckhorn on any lonely night
You may see a pretty lady in a flowing dress of white.
She'll accept a ride you offer and bid you "drive with care"
Then when you stop to let her out, you'll find she isn't there;
She searches still for the love she lost a hundred years ago.
Oh, shake your head and laugh or scoff but those who have seen her know.

The legend says they planned to wed one April day
At dawn, with lover's eagerness, he started on his way.
Along that Buckhorn road he urged his horse to utmost speed,
It stumbled, reared and he was trampled beneath his steed.
His pain was great, but he tried, so valiantly, to rise.
He called her name with his last breath, and then he closed his eyes.

At that same time, his bride-elect was busy in her room,
Bathing, combing, dressing joyously to meet her groom.
Arrayed at last, she saw the time and realized he was late.
She thought "I'll walk to meet him. I can't just sit here and wait."
She didn't think to take a coat, and no one saw her go;
A little later, it turned cold, and then began to snow -

Both dead! And they were laid to rest, forever, side by side,
But she's so wrapped up in her search, she doesn't know she died!
Mindless of passing time she walks along that Buckhorn trail
Wrapped in the folds of her fine lace shawl she chose for a bridal veil.
She searches still for the love she lost and hundred years ago.
Oh shake your head and laugh or scoff, but WE who have seen her KNOW!

>*<

Turn around and come down off the mountain. After Route 36 becomes 18th Street once again, keep an eye out for 9th Avenue. A left onto 9th Avenue will bring us to the haunted Mishler Theater.

The Mishler Theater

1208 12th Avenue
Altoona

Isaac "Doc" Mishler was an impresario who built, rebuilt, owned, and operated theaters in Johnstown and Altoona in Pennsylvania as well as in Trenton, New Jersey. Theater was his life and he loved it. He leased the 11th Avenue Opera House in Altoona during 1894. He also controlled the Opera House in Johnstown until it was destroyed by fire in 1903. In 1895 he bought the Cambria Theater in Johnstown which had fallen upon hard times after the Great Flood of 1889. He also built the State Street Theater in Trenton, NJ opening it with "Mary of Magdala" starring Mrs. Fiske.

But, his passion was for the Mishler Theater on 12th Avenue in Altoona. He had it designed by the famous theatrical architect Albert E. Westover, built it at a cost of $115,000 and was so satisfied with it that it became his flagship theater bearing his name.

The Mishler opened its doors on February 15, 1906 with a performance of "Merely Mary Ann" starring Eleanor Robson. Eight months later the theater was destroyed by fire, but Doc Mishler was undaunted and rebuilt it in less than a year. Over the next few decades, The Mishler Theater was host to all the luminaries of the stage and screen, including W. C. Fields, Al Jolson, and Houdini. Both The Ziegfield Follies and the John Phillip Sousa Band performed there. Even heavyweight boxers Jack Johnson and Jack Dempsey demonstrated their pugilistic skills there.

As with all long-lasting theatrical enterprises, The Mishler fell upon hard times after its great early success, having an incarnation as a movie house for years, and was even threatened with the wrecker's ball at one point during the 1960s. Then just like the fabled Phoenix, it literally rose from the ashes once again and, like a cat with nine-lives, it was reincarnated, restored, reborn, and came full circle to its original halcyon days, even being placed on the National Register of Historical Places in 1973.

Isaac "Doc" Mishler passed on in 1944 at the age of 82, but loved his theater so much that he has remained there ever since. Many people over the years including actors, directors, stage hands, support staff, and visitors have encountered his benevolent spirit at various places throughout the theater. Smelling and even seeing smoke from his ever present trademark cigar is commonplace among them. But no encounter has even been as vivid as those experienced by young Madeline Lesche. She recalls that when she was barely more than a toddler accompanying her mother who was a backstage worker at the theater, a kindly older gentleman befriended her and would walk with her and talk with her as she explored all the interesting places to play there. She especially remembered the many different, often funny hats he wore during their visits. The man she described perfectly fit the picture of Isaac Mishler.

The sounds of a howling dog have echoed throughout the building, even when there are no opera productions in rehearsal and one of the ladies restrooms is a particular hot spot for haunts. A woman in Victorian garb adjusts her make-up at the mirror there only to disappear when approached and the faucets turn on and off at will accompanied by random flushing of the toilets. Persons dressed in clothing of the early 1900s turn up in photographs taken in the theater when nobody should have been there.

The theater was even featured in an episode of the popular Television series, *Ghost Hunters* and at least one employee, Technical Director Brian McConnell has had so many paranormal experiences in the place that he refuses to be there alone, unless a door is propped open.

1,000 feet away as the crow flies is the Altoona Railroaders Memorial Museum. We don't fly as the crows do, so we have to drive the distance. Just head south on 12th Avenue to 17th Street, take a left onto 17th, travel a few blocks and turn left on 9th Avenue. The museum will be on our left by 13th Street.

Altoona Railroaders Memorial Museum

1300 9th. Avenue
Altoona, PA

Altoona's nickname is Railroad City, and no small wonder that it is. It is situated right where a major east to west railroad corridor intersects with a major north to south one. The world famous Horseshoe Curve that made it possible for the Ohio River Valley to become an international industrial leader was built just outside of town. And, even before that, the Pennsylvania Canal and Portage Railroad system ran just south of the city. And, for over 100 years, Altoona was one of the world's most important rail centers employing over 15,000 persons and being the home of the largest rail shop complex on the globe. It has railroading in its civic blood.

It is only fitting that it now has the nation's only interactive railroader's museum. It is located in the 100+ year old former headquarters building of the Pennsylvania Railroad police. The building also served as an infirmary for injured and sick railroaders for a time.

With this kind of history, it comes as no surprise that it is haunted by the shades of former railroad workers. EVPs have been collected by paranormal investigators in the building at night when nobody is there. These EVPs are of big band music, the favorite of the railroaders during the 1930s and 40s.

One ghost is of a man who climbs to the top of the museum's centerpiece, a replica of Pennsylvania Rail Road Steam Locomotive Number 1341. Once he gets there, he fades from existence. Other times he has been spotted walking alongside the locomotive, only to disappear when you try to bring his visage into focus. He has been spotted so many times that he has been identified and even given a name. The ghost is of a young, small-statured man who is in the center of a photograph of a 1920s boiler crew on display in the museum. Although nobody knows his name for sure, he has been dubbed "Frank" by employees of the facility.

He's not the only one there. Surveillance cameras have monitored the existence and activities of people who weren't there. At least one person exhibiting suspicious activity disappeared before the eyes of the person watching the monitor as the security staff arrived to intercept him. A customer of the store reported another man wearing out-of-date clothing who vanished just as he was about to ask him a question. Even Executive

Director Scott Cessna has had encounters with the haunts, sharing an elevator ride with one of them on at least one occasion.

Spend some time there enjoying the rich railroading history of the area and just maybe, you will run into someone who looks as though they have stepped out of that history. If you do, pay attention, for they will probably vanish as quickly as they appeared.

After leaving the museum you might want to walk over to the 12th Street bridge. Over there, people have seen a person leaping from the bridge onto the tops of passing railroad trains only to disappear as their feet contact those trains. Strange, huh?

Had enough of this work-a-day other-worldliness? Let's take a little jaunt to visit with the hoi-poloi that's only a mile away in distance, but an immeasurable distance in class and society. The headquarters of the Blair County Historical Society lies within the palatial Baker Mansion on Oak Lane. Elias Baker and his family make today's top one percenters look like paupers. They deserve a visit from us.

A little zig-zagging will get us there. Let's head back on 9th Street, take a left on 17th Avenue, a right onto Route 764, a left onto Union Avenue which also happens to be Route 36, a right onto Crescent, and finally a left onto Oak Lane. Whew! Five turns in less than two miles! The imposing edifice brooding over you on the hill to your right is our destination.

The Baker Mansion

**3419 Oak Lane
Altoona**

This historic home built between 1844 and 1848 has been operated as a museum by the Blair County Historical Society since 1922. The society eventually purchased the mansion and it has been its headquarters since 1941. The Baker family has a real and everlasting attachment to the mansion and has stayed on, even after death.

Elias Baker made his fortune with the Allaghany Furnace nearby producing iron daily by the tens of tons. His first house, near the furnace was described by him as, "a tolerable good mansion," but it just wasn't up to the standards that he had set for raising a family. So, he caused the opulent, ostentatious Baker Mansion to be designed by Baltimore architect Robert Carey Long, Jr. and built on Oak Lane. The three story Greek Revival style building took nearly 5 years to construct from 1844 to 1849. Approaching the main entrance, one gets the feeling that early Athenians must have gotten when entering the Parthenon for the first time. You almost expect to see the statue of Zeus in a place of honor. It is difficult to imagine people actually living a day-to-day existence among all this splendor. Live there they did, and all because Elias Baker would stand for nothing less than the absolute finest in all things for his family.

When his daughter Anna met, fell in love with, and asked permission to marry a common iron worker, Elias Baker went ballistic. He had raised his daughter as befitting a princess. And his little princess was in no way, shape, or form going to marry a commoner. He put his foot down, refused permission for the marriage and absolutely forbade Anna to ever see the love of her young life again. She acquiesced to her father's demands and broke it off with her suitor. However, knowing that she would never meet anyone who could replace that young man in her heart, she never formed any relationship with another man for the balance of her life. She died a spinster in 1914.

Anna had been so sure of her father's permission that, before she even asked for his permission to marry, she had hand crafted for her a wedding dress that could only exist in a princess' dreams. For only a royal family could afford such a garment. It was never to be worn by its intended. The daughter of another wealthy nearby family did wear it for *her* wedding. Elizabeth Bell is rumored to have mocked Anna for never marrying while wearing the dress designed for Anna to the altar. The fabulous dress was on display for many years at the museum, gathering the name, "The haunted Bell wedding dress," over the years.

Anna was finally granted her wish to wear her wedding dress. Only it came long after she had passed away. For years, visitors and staff at the museum were treated to watching the dress turning first this way, then that in its display behind protective glass. Many explanations were offered for this seemingly inexplicable event ranging from loose floorboards to stray breezes. Of course there are no loose floorboards in the fortress-constructed mansion and likewise, there are no breezes inside the glass case. The consensus of opinion is that it is Anna herself trying on the dress and preening in it, trying to decide which view is most flattering. In death, she has accomplished what she couldn't in life – wearing her wedding gown.

Anna isn't alone rattling around in the huge edifice, she is accompanied by other members of her family starting with her brother, David, who passed from this earthly pale in 1852. He was 28 years old at the time and had been enjoying himself as a moneyed crew member of a steamer. As a result of an accident while pursuing that avocation during the winter he died and was brought home for the funeral. It was the dead of winter and the ground was frozen solid so that no graves could be dug. David's equally frozen lifeless body was placed in an unheated area within the mansion's basement to await the spring thaw when he could be properly buried. He has been seen from time-to-time in the vicinity of the basement wearing clothing similar to that worn by steamboat crew members of that era. One youngster on a visit to the museum refused to enter the basement, saying that there was a soldier standing at the bottom of the stairs. He probably mistook David's seafaring clothing for a military uniform.

Elias himself prefers the dining room, sometimes enjoying an after dinner cigar that is smelled wafting on the air of the elegant room. Anna spends some of her afterlife in the parlor and upstairs bedrooms, refusing to socialize with her father even into eternity.

Her older brother Sylvester, who took over the family business and finances after Elias' death in 1864, also never married, remaining a bachelor for life, spending all his years in the family mansion. Like any old curmudgeon, he craves attention and bangs away on the floor with his cane until he becomes the center of attention. Once he gets that attention, he is satisfied and becomes quiet once again.

What of Elias' wife Hetty? The matriarch of this wonderfully dysfunctional but wealthy family is not allowed to rest peacefully either. Wearing the heavy black dress of mourning, she is seen roaming the hallways and rooms of the second floor, perhaps wondering if all her family's sadness is the fault of one man who was determined to make his little clan into a bit of Industrial Age royalty.

And it is all accompanied by the mournful tinkling of a mystical music box commenting on this sad state of affairs at random times and with no outside influence.

That chill you feel isn't the result of a stray breeze blowing over a grave ... or is it?

>*<

You know what contributes to a chill? How about a ride on a haunted roller coaster? OK, get back on Crescent Rd. by retracing your way on Oak Lane and turning right. Turn right onto South Union Ave./PA Route 36. Bear left onto Frankstown Rd., cross over the Interstate and turn right onto Park Avenue, and you've arrived at Lakemont Park and The Island Water Park. Get ready for a great few hours with a minimal outlay of money.

Lakemont Park

700 Park Avenue
Altoona

People come to Lakemont Park in Altoona from all over the world to ride the world's oldest surviving wooden roller coaster, Leap the Dips. A classic trolley park, Lakemont Park is a great way to spend an inexpensive day in these times of overpriced everything. Even on weekends, an all-inclusive ride ticket that gives admission to its water park cost less than ten dollars in 2013. However, due to the expensive upkeep of the antique Leap the Dips, it isn't included in the general admission price. That'll cost you another $2.50, but it's worth it, just to be able to say that you rode the world's oldest wooden roller coaster.

Over at the northern end of the park, dominating the skyline overlooking the new Altoona Curve Baseball Team's stadium lies another wooden roller coaster. The Skyliner. If it's just roller coaster thrills you're interested in, this may be more your cup of tea. It was transported here lock, stock, and barrel from New York's Roseland Park where it had been thrilling riders for many years.

On a sad note, a maintenance worker who was responsible for the daily inspection of the rides was struck by one of the cars on one of the roller coasters and he fell many feet below to the ground suffering fatal injuries. The particular roller coaster is not named but, the ancient Leap the Dips, along with the Steel Toboggan built in 1971 are the suspects.

Notwithstanding that, he has been seen on all three coasters. Riders have reported to ride staff about the maintenance worker they have seen along the track while they are riding, obviously feeling that this is an extremely unsafe practice. Imagine their surprise when told by the ride operators that there are no maintenance staff on the ride at that time. Did they see the departed ride inspector trying to finish his interrupted rounds? Take a ride yourself. Maybe you'll see him as well.

Lets take a short jaunt over to Hollidaysburg which is the home of a hotel that is crammed to overflowing with ghosts. Heading through Hollidaysburg via Route 22, keep a watch for Wayne Street on your right. The U. S. Hotel is located where Wayne Street ends at Juniata Street. Take a good look at this place and be transported back to a rough and tumble time on the frontier.

Ed Kelemen

~III~
The Juniata River Valley

Home of The

Pennsylvania Canal Main Line

The U.S. Hotel

**401 South Juniata Street
Hollidaysburg**

When the Allegheny Portage Railroad section of the Pennsylvania Canal opened the west to two-way commerce and passenger traffic in 1834, it brought a myriad of opportunity for the enterprising businessman. John Dougherty was just that kind of a businessman.

The Pennsylvania Canal basin, actually a large manmade lake, was created in Hollidaysburg as a parking lot for the canal boats. The canal boats heading west to Pittsburgh sat bobbing in the basin waiting their turn to experience the exciting ride up and over the Allegheny Mountains along the Portage Railroad. Boats heading east waited for the mule teams to start the four-day journey east.

This meant that there were a lot of people hanging around with time on their hands, money in their pockets, dry throats, and a rumbling in their stomach. The noise of the celebration opening the final link in the canal had barely stopped echoing in the valley when the newly built U.S. Hotel opened for business in 1835. Travelers, canal men, teamsters, merchants, and railroaders now had a first-class place to sip, sup, and stay over while waiting to make connections at this new crossroads of commerce that was Hollidaysburg.

Under the management of John Dougherty, the U.S. Hotel thrived for the entire 20 years that the Pennsylvania Canal was in existence. Unlike other establishments that depended on canal traffic, the U.S. Hotel continued to thrive long after the canal's demise. It was ideally situated to adapt to changing conditions, and it rode the railroad boom for another 100 years.

Its long road wasn't without bumps, however. In 1871 a fire rushed through the building. The conflagration destroyed the building, but not the spirit of the hotel. It took nearly a decade and a half, but German emigrant Englebert Gromiller not only rebuilt it and reopened in 1886, he added a brewery next door. In later years, the building was allowed to lie fallow with little maintenance and less in the way of improvements. It started showing its age and changed hands many times. The brewery became unprofitable and was demolished.(How can a brewery be unprofitable?) The old dowager was rescued by the Yoders and restored to the finery of its glory days, only to fall on hard times once again. It is currently closed and for sale. But I have no doubt that it will return to take its rightful place as a piece of our history.

During this past century and three quarters, the U.S. Hotel has been host to all kinds of people from all walks of life, so it is no surprise that it hosts denizens from the other side who are equally diverse. There is such an overcrowding of otherworldly inhabitants in this venerable building that it is hard to understand how they can coexist without intruding on one another's personal space.

Famous medium, psychic, author, and paranormal investigator Patty Wilson came face to face with her very first full-bodied apparition in one of the upstairs rooms. A young lady with chestnut hair was sitting on a bed, her lower half covered by a brown blanket. She held her head in her hands and writhed back and forth in anguish, her beautiful hair a disheveled, tangled mess. Patty emphatically shared her pain and turned away to regain control. When she turned back, the bed was empty.

During that visit, Patty and her team encountered an evil shadow man who exhibited intense hatred for the woman, shouting about the "bitch" over and over again on EVPs. Another spirit, whom Patty felt was the young woman with the chestnut hair, implored them to "Run, get out of here!" And the paranormal investigators were followed home. That despicable entity was seen in at least one of their bedrooms and inflicted on them intense headaches and debilitating nightmares.

Although the more expensive wines were kept under lock and key in a solid cabinet, the owner of the hotel says that on many occasions she has locked the cabinet at night only to find it in the morning with the door wide open and one or two bottles removed from their niches. But there is never any wine missing. Another ghost appears so often that they have given her the name Sarah just because, one staffer put it, "She looks like her name should be Sarah."

A floating "lady in white" haunts the second floor. She floats along about a foot and a half above the floor with no feet visible. She doesn't engage anyone in any manner. She just appears, floats along, and disappears. It's almost like watching a video loop.

Other spirits include a young boy sitting on the front staircase. Don't bother to ask him what he's doing there; he'll disappear before you get an answer. A specter thought to be a poltergeist runs about the third floor, ax in hand, ready to do who knows what.

Unseen celebrations are held upstairs when there is nobody there, accompanied by the tinkling of stemware and the clatter of dishes. One time, the building manager was leaving for the night when he heard that celebration. He got to his car only to realize that he'd left his car keys inside, so he returned. Opening the front door, he discovered that the party had moved downstairs to the barroom. He got his keys and left the unseen revelers to party the night away.

We will do likewise and head on east to the Royer Mansion, where a gracious hostess who passed on more than a half-century ago may offer us a tour of her former home. About 15 minutes east on Route 22 is PA Route

866. Turn on PA 866 toward Williamsburg. Drive through this quaint rural town. About three miles south of town is the Royer Mansion on our left, serenely surrounded by trees, shrubbery, and flowers.

The Royer Mansion

3909 Piney Creek Road
Williamsburg

The Royers were yet another Pennsylvania family who made their fortune with the abundant iron ore and other materials necessary for the production of iron. In 1812 John Royer built the Cove Forge. Three years later he partnered with his brother Daniel and built the Springfield Furnace to provide iron to the Cove Forge and the Franklin Forge, which belonged to his other brother, Samuel.

First shipping iron bars by horseback, then the Main Line Pennsylvania Canal, then the Pennsylvania Railroad, the Royers sent their high-grade Juniata iron over the mountains to the Pittsburgh market.

Samuel Royer built a house along Piney Creek Road

south of Williamsburg in that beautiful pastoral valley between two ridges of the Allegheny Mountains. Unfortunately, it burned to the ground. The family lost everything. But, as the demand for iron restored the family's fortunes, the beautiful Royer Mansion rose over the ashes of the previous building in 1815. Six years later, Samuel Royer and his bride, Sarah, purchased the mansion and moved in. It ever after carried the Royer family name. Sarah gave birth to six children in that house before passing away in 1832. The widower Samuel remarried and his second wife, Martha, provided him with four more children. Samuel expanded the mansion and, to all accounts, lived a happy existence there until dying at the age of 64 in 1856.

The next person of note to live there was Carrie Hartman, wife of one of Samuel's grandsons. She lived in the mansion until she died within its walls in 1965.

And then the hauntings started, or at least became common knowledge.

The most intense took place at the spring-house next to the main building. A visitor walking the grounds heard children playing in the creek near the spring house. Strolling in that direction, he saw a few youngsters dressed in what he describes as "old-fashioned clothing." One was a little boy of three or four years who clambered down the slope to the stream that feeds the spring-house. Now, even though there is a fence around that area today, the witness didn't see one. He did hear screams. He saw a woman retrieve the child's lifeless body from the waters of the stream, sobbing uncontrollably all the while. Then she disappeared.

Investigation turned up no record of a child drowning at the mansion. Of course, records from the first half of the 19th century are neither reliable nor all that available today. Perhaps an account of this tragedy is tucked away in an as-yet-undiscovered family Bible somewhere in the valley.

Another time, two high school students arrived at the mansion to meet a member of the Blair County Historical Society who was going to conduct a private tour for them. They were writing a paper on the history of the mansion. There was no car parked nearby, but the door was answered by a gracious older lady who welcomed them in and showed them around. They described her as very helpful and full of information about the mansion.

The lady had one disquieting quirk. She constantly talked to someone who wasn't there and carried on a conversation that wasn't pertinent to the questions the girls asked. They became so uneasy that they felt compelled to make a hasty exit from the mansion without even saying thanks and good-bye.

When the mother of one of the girls heard about their hasty retreat, she called the historical society to offer her apology for the girls' rudeness. Imagine the mother's consternation when the woman from the historical society instead offered *her* apology for missing her appointment with the girls.

From the girls' description of their tour guide and her clothing, the only likely explanation was that they had been treated to a tour by none other than Carrie Hartman herself – who had been dead for over half a century.

Inside the mansion, tread carefully and keep your hand on the banister when you use the stairs. A ghost who hangs out there will exert just enough pressure to put you off balance. You wouldn't want to fall down those nearly 200-year old steps, would you?

Many people have an indefinable feeling of being watched when they are on the grounds, and at least one person has taken a picture of a rogue mist arising from the stream near the spring-house.

On our way back the six miles to Route 22, take a look at the structures and maybe you will be able to see what I haven't been able to see: the site of a feed mill that is haunted by the plaintive wails of a baby. Read on to find out about the feed-mill baby.

The Infant Ghost of the Feed Mill
Williamsburg, PA

The plaintive sounds of a baby crying were heard coming from the cellar of a house in the town of Williamsburg. No amount of searching down there could find the poor thing, and the owners were baffled. Years went by and the home was sold to a businessman who converted it into a feed mill. While digging out the old sewer lines to replace them, the owner found a burlap bag. Inside it were the remains of an infant. So goes the story of this haunting.

But I have been able to identify only two feed mills in the general Williamsburg area, neither of which is a transformed house. And the only reference I can find to this story is an online one without location, date, or substantiation. So unless someone who reads this book can furnish verifiable information, I'm chalking it up to overactive imaginations and folklore.

Back up on the main road of Route 22 heading east, let's visit a tavern, restaurant, and inn that has been sitting on the bank of the Frankstown Branch of the Juniata River for more than 250 years. It was once owned by a grandson of William Penn and has been a witness to the development of our country since before it was even a country. Some of the thousands of patrons and employees who have supped and sipped at this historic inn must have decided to stay on long after their earthly remains ceased to exist.

Come on. After you pass the town of Alexandria and turn onto River Road, it's just about a mile along the road on the left.

The Inn at Edgewater Acres

7653 Edgewater Acres Road
Alexandria

John Penn was the grandson of William Penn, the founder and namesake of the Commonwealth of Pennsylvania. It is no wonder that he fell in love with this beautiful pastoral place nestled among silent sentinel evergreens along the bank of the placidly flowing Juniata River. Just slowly riding up the driveway to the 250-year old inn is a leisurely travel back in time to a more tranquil existence. The white wooden rockers on the stone-floored porch just beg to be used to while away an afternoon. It takes little imagination to picture John Penn rocking gently in one of those chairs, a mug of ale at hand and his clay pipe dribbling smoke.

Not exactly a prime location for ghostly activity? On the contrary, this building is home to a number of haunts, seen and unseen.

Several people, including one of the owners, have seen shadowy figures flit by at the edge of their vision, just out of focus. It is a practice at the inn to set the tables in the dining room before closing for the night. Owner Debra Sassure told City Lights Paranormal Society that she has often found the next morning that the silverware has been rearranged by somebody or something during the night.

Customers and staff alike have heard the tread of footsteps across the second-story floorboards when no one is on the second floor. Conversation between a woman and a man is heard in those upstairs rooms when there is nobody there – at least nobody who can be seen.

On the first floor, someone can be heard speaking in the vicinity of the fireplace, which is part of the original 2-room log cabin that started all this history. Although the voice is clearly a woman's, her words are indecipherable.

The City Lights Paranormal Society conducted an in-depth, mulch-team investigation in the spring of 2010. The results were phenomenal. Electronic voice recorders set up in strategic locations caught ten separate instances of disembodied voices, ranging from pleas for help to orders to leave. Members of the society encountered voices, shuffling noises, raps, banging, and blasts of air. They even witnessed an apparition.

So drive up the wonderful driveway to this historic pre-Revolutionary War inn, park your car, and sit at the bar in a genuinely haunted inn. If you hear the lady over at the fireplace speaking, listen closely. Maybe you will be the first to understand what she is saying. Take advantage of the dining room's wonderful offerings and stay the night with a full belly. As you drift off in one of those comfortable beds, listen for late-night conversations between people who aren't there.

Back on Route 22 heading east we'll encounter Huntington about seven miles along the road. Huntington was the home of a prolific 19th-century author who has lingered, perhaps seeking more plot twists for her fiction. Or is it fiction?

The Gypsy Wild House
Huntingdon

Huntingdon was home to an author who went by a number of names during her career, including Gypsy Wild. She was a quite colorful type, living the bohemian lifestyle and raising less liberal eyebrows all around her. In the heart of Union sympathies, she is rumored to have taken a Confederate soldier from Virginia as a lover shortly after the Battle of Gettysburg. Of course, for this rumor to be true, she would have to have been precocious; she was only 16 years old at the time!

La Dolce Vita finally wore thin and Gypsy Wild settled down, married a local doctor, and blended in with the society around her.

Most of her books and stories were written under her actual name, Linda M. Sangree, or her married name, Linda M. Sangree Allen. She published at least three novels. *Mignonnette* was issued in 1885, followed by *The Devil and I* in 1889 and *Florine* in 1891. These were all written while she was in her late 30s and early 40s. She wrote for weeks on end cloistered in the tower that is part of the house she called home, receiving her meals via dumbwaiter provided by her sister.

In 1929, at the age of 82, she felt a premonition that her days had come to an end. She picked out her favorite red dress and put it on, painted her nails, did her hair, and then lay down on her bed. Next she smiled, crossed her arms on her bosom, closed her eyes, and died.

Three quarters of a century later, another writer, Michelle by name, found and fell in love with Mrs. Sangree-Allen's home. The garret tower was guaranteed to appeal to the romantic spirit of any author. Michelle and her husband bought the house and moved in with their seven-year old son.

What followed was a paranormal adventure that cemented their love affair with the home. Their son acquired an otherworldly playmate named Jacob. When Michelle was counting off steps to measure a room, her count was interrupted by an unseen spirit who disagreed with her measurement. Neighbors wave to a lady on the porch who shouldn't be there, and the face of a woman appears in one of the windows. Disembodied voices abound. Once when Michelle was fumbling to unlock the front door, a helpful spirit in the empty house turned on the porch light so she could see to insert the key.

Lewistown is a leisurely drive along this venerable highway through alternating plains, meadows, and mountains. Turn up the stereo, kick back, and enjoy the next five minutes of our trip until we reach that crossroads city.

The Haunts of Lewistown

Lewistown Town Square

Geez- Lewistown, PA seems like such a nice little city situated as it is on a bend of the meandering Juniata River as it heads to the Susquehanna River 45 miles or so to the east. Hidden under that serene exterior lies a hotbed of hauntings.

>*<

The former Green Gables Hotel at 900 South Main Street on Route 22's original path was *the* place to stay, wine, and dine since it opened in 1931 to serve travelers with 22 rooms and a fine restaurant. In 1966 an additional 20 rooms were added due to its popularity and location. Unfortunately over the next half-century it fell on hard times brought on by economics, a 4-lane bypass that no longer funnels traffic through town, and chain hotels and motels that offer both a less interesting and less expensive experience. It is now no longer in business.

And that's a shame, since it was, and probably still is, host to a number of entities that have refused to cross over. Kitchen staff constantly suffered aggravation at the hands of a mischievous ghost that liked to move things around just to make it difficult for them to do their job. And not just little things like ladles, serving spoons, spatulas, and mixing bowls. Nope, it was stronger than that, it even moved smaller appliances, garbage cans, and stools. Employees entering the walk-in cooler to get supplies have been told by an unseen, but heard person who whispers in a decidedly feminine voice to, "Turn off the lights." Maybe she could do something that the living couldn't - see in the dark.

A skinny black fellow who goes by the name of George appears and fades from sight on the second floor of the 1966 addition as well as in the parking lot.

A pair of youngsters liked to hang out in the vicinity of the main lobby, sometimes interacting with travelers who were there to request a room for the night. When a patron would comment about them at the check-in counter, the clerk would inform the hapless customer that there were no children present.

Finally, there was the roaming banquet cart that would turn up anywhere except where it was supposed to be. The kitchen ghost probably had something to do with that.

The former Dr. F. W. Black Hospital was the location of the Mifflin Juniata Area Agency on Aging until May 2013. It was a place of numerous staff interruptions caused by unexplained music, faint conversations just on the edge of understandability, and the sound of a baby crying. Supervisors tried to explain away the sounds with both fact and fantasy, all to no avail. And the workers were glad to see the last of that place when they moved to new digs elsewhere in Lewistown.

Heritage Gardens Flowers and Gifts on Ort Valley Road is another such place with a history of weird happenings that go back 60-plus years. The back room is where most of the activity takes place. Boxes slide across the floor, balls of light dart hither and yon in the workroom, and loud voices are heard back there when the room is empty. The general consensual of opinion of the owners, employees, and paranormal investigators who have checked the place out is that it is haunted by a female presence with an impudent sense of humor, a joker.

At least one local family tempted fate by moving into a house that they knew in advance was haunted. Skeptics then, believers now. Before they had even settled into their new home their daughter encountered a "masked apparition" that wanted her to come into a closet with it. This was followed with voices, screams, objects flying through the air, and water being turned on and off. There were loud knocks and rapping at all hours of the day and night and the door bell would spontaneously ring at odd hours with no one at the door. Nothing the family has done has been able to get rid of the hauntings. Neither paranormal investigators nor a cleric's blessings have had any effect. And the events continue. The family still lives in this house and I have neither identified them nor the address of their home for obvious reasons.

One place I will identify and tell you to watch for a possible ghost is that portion of U.S. Route 322 that shares its way with Route 22 between Lewistown and Harrisburg. It may save you from getting hoof prints on your hood.

General "Mad Anthony" Wayne's Bones

Along Old Route 22

Allow me to share with you a story about a hero named General Anthony Wayne. General Wayne earned the nickname "Mad Anthony" during his career as a leader of troops during the Revolutionary War. There are a number of explanations for how he got his name. I prefer the ones that highlight his valor in battle.

General Wayne had a penchant for getting himself and his troops into situations that would baffle and dismay other general officers who had less bravery, faith in themselves and their soldiers, charisma, and just plain old Pennsylvania guts. He convinced General George Washington that, with just the equivalent of one small, unsupported light infantry regiment of about 1,500 men, he could capture the supposedly impregnable British fort at Stony Point, New York. This fort was garrisoned with 500 men and protected on three sides by water and on the fourth by a swamp. Furthermore, it sat 150 feet above the Hudson River near West Point, was equipped with heavy artillery, and had a commanding view all about it.

Armed with surprise and little else, General Wayne's troops attacked before sunrise on July 16, 1779. The battle lasted a mere 30 minutes. When it was over the Americans had captured the fort with a loss of 15 killed and 83 wounded. The British had 94 killed and wounded and 472 captured. But surmounting those impossible odds wasn't what earned him his nickname. No, what earned him his nickname was that he did it all with a BAYONET CHARGE. Mad indeed.

He was so popular that, after he visited an inn on the outskirts of Philadelphia with some of his men for a weekend of revelry, the innkeeper renamed the inn in his honor. For more than 200 years, until the inn closed its doors once and for all, it was known as the General Wayne Inn. That inn was a paranormal oddity in its own right, harboring more than eighteen ghosts within its walls.

By the time the Revolutionary War came to an end, General Wayne had attained the rank of major general. He then served as commander in chief of the United States Army under President Washington, distinguished himself in frontier wars out West, and died at Fort Presque Isle in Erie, Pennsylvania He was buried in a place of honor at the base of the fort's flagpole. The year was 1796. He was only 51 years old, and he left behind two children, Margretta and Isaac.

For 13 years, Margretta whined, cajoled, and generally nagged Isaac that it was not right for their father's remains to be buried so far from home. He deserved better and should be buried in a consecrated church cemetery. Since it appeared to Isaac that she was never going to let up on her campaign, he finally agreed to go get dear old Dad's body and bring it back to Philadelphia for a proper burial.

Isaac set off on horseback to Erie, some 400 miles away, to complete the quest forced on him by the insistent Margretta. He expected that after 13 years (without embalming) there would be little left of his father's body beyond a few bones and some rotten fabric. Imagine his consternation when, upon disinterring dear old Dad, he found that the body was largely intact. He hadn't enough room on his horse for a body. Besides, 400 miles with a rotting corpse bouncing behind him in a bedroll wasn't the way he wanted to travel. He came up with a solution: boil the meat off Dad's bones.

He plopped the body into a cauldron, added water, and brought the soup to a boil. No mention of onions, potatoes, and carrots was made. It boiled until all the meat separated from the bones. No mention is made about the fate of the meat, either. Was it reburied? Fed to dogs? Thrown away? And what happened to the broth?

Isaac took his dad's bones, put them in a pair of saddlebags, and rode east for Philadelphia. Maybe he wasn't all that comfortable with his dad's bones so close to him on the horse. Maybe he rode a little faster than was absolutely necessary. In any case, when he got to Philadelphia, he had fewer bones in the saddlebags than when he departed Erie. Various and sundry of his father's bones, constantly jostled in overfull saddlebags, had fallen out along the road that has become U.S. Route 322.

Still, enough bones remained that an appropriate ceremony, one that satisfied his sister's sensibilities, was held. General "Mad" Anthony Wayne was duly interred in the Wayne family plot at Saint David's Episcopal Church in Radnor, only six miles from the inn that bore his name.

Anthony Wayne was larger than life when he shared this Earth with us mere mortals, and he continued his flamboyance into the afterlife. Something as mundane as a grave can't confine him, not when he has a quest to complete. He can't rest until all his bones have been reunited in one grave. Every New Year's Day finds him galloping the length of U.S. 322 atop his wonderful warhorse, in full uniform, as befits a Revolutionary War general.

So if you find yourself driving that length of U.S. 22 that shares its route with U.S. 322 between Lewistown and Harrisburg on any given January 1 and see a madman rushing toward you on horseback, it isn't your imagination playing tricks on you. Neither is it a product of over imbibing spirituous libations when welcoming the New Year. Nope, it's General " Mad" Anthony Wayne frantically searching for his missing parts on the one day a year that he can do so. Drive carefully.

While looking for Mad Anthony atop his warhorse, you may notice after crossing the Susquehanna River an exit for PA Route 443, also called Fishing Valley Road. Crossing over the U.S. 22/322 expressway will bring you to a little lane on the left called Cemetery Road. Unless you have a desire to get some dust on the side of your car, don't waste your time at Mummy Hill Cemetery.

This small, nondescript cemetery is reputed to be rife with medium to large orbs that flash into and out of existence and travel rapidly through the area. I have not been able to find any verifiable report of this. Furthermore, when I personally checked it out, I saw no evidence of paranormal activity at this location. It seems to be nothing more than the local lore that attaches itself to almost every cemetery. I would like to be proven wrong, but for the time being, I'm going with my previous statement. Don't waste your time here.

Instead, continue along U.S. 22/322 eastward and take the U.S. 15 North/U.S. 11 North Exit toward Selingsgrove. As you are sweeping round to the right, keep an eye out for River Road and turn onto it. Here is insanity and tragedy, compounded by criminal stupidity.

Amity Hall Hotel

River Road
Duncannon,

The Amity Hall Hotel opened for business in the early 1830s to serve the people who traveled the Pennsylvania Canal. It was a stately building. A welcoming covered porch ran across the front of the three-story brick federal-style building. Huge fireplaces at either end provided warmth as well as heat for cooking for most of its first 100 years.

When the Pennsylvania Canal went out of business, the hotel continued to prosper, serving the clientele of the railroads that took over from it. During the Civil War, it was a hospital for wounded and convalescing soldiers.

As the 20th century progressed, the revenue provided by railroad commerce was first supplemented, then replaced by motorists who preferred car travel to trains. Then the U.S. 322/22 limited-access highway bypassed the rural spot known as Amity Hall. That marked the beginning of the end. The Amity Hall Hotel closed its doors forever. It lay empty for 20 years, give or take, until May 19, 2009.

The hotel was the scene of many life-altering events, like any structure open to the public for over two centuries. Babies were born here. Soldiers passed away from their war injuries here. Marriages were celebrated within the walls, and wakes were held here. Charitable acts as well as criminal ones took place on the property.

One that left an indelible mark was a horrific murder-suicide that eradicated an entire family. A man's descent into madness led him to beat his wife to death and leave her lifeless body on the blood-soaked front porch. He then went upstairs to where his children were asleep and bludgeoned them to death. Perhaps a spark of sanity flashed across his consciousness and he realized what he had done. Stricken with remorse, he took his own life.

After that act of violence, customers would encounter the ghost of a woman on the second floor who exuded intense hatred for men. It was supposed that she was the murdered wife, confusing all men with the one who killed her and her babies. Sourceless blue lights flit and fly about that second floor as well. And small, dark, indescribable creatures occupy the copse of trees in and around the parking lot, bringing feelings of intense dread with them. These so-called imps may be the spirits of the murdered children, trying to escape their inescapable fate. A mournful woman's face appears at one of the attic dormer windows, staring off into space until she fades from sight. Is this the mother too, or a ghost with her own story?

The hauntings are no longer witnessed, as the hotel, alas, is no more. The abandoned building became a mecca for unauthorized so-called ghost hunters looking for a thrill, even though it was festooned with "No Trespassing" signs. Signs don't stop criminals, and the trespassing continued until a 12-foot tall chain link fence was built around the old hotel. Even this didn't stop a bunch of lowlifes who pushed down a portion of that fence, trespassed in the building, and set a fire that consumed it on May 19, 2009.

Thirteen fire companies responded to the conflagration; 80 firefighters risked their lives as the building collapsed in upon itself. Eight young men were arrested and charged with arson, criminal trespass, criminal mischief, and conspiracy. They were sent to jail for various terms and ordered to pay restitution of nearly a quarter of a million dollars. It's too bad they couldn't have learned that "No Trespassing" means no trespassing without mortgaging their future.

Now the once-proud building is a destroyed hulk visible through the reinforced chain link fence that surrounds it. Even so, a sense of foreboding lingers in the parking area outside that fence.

Heading east on Routes 22/322 once more, we will cross the great Susquehanna River in a mile or so and enter Harrisburg, Pennsylvania's capital, another 15 miles along the road. Just stay on Route 22/322 as it

enters Harrisburg. U.S. 322 will end and Route 22 will follow the path of Cameron Street. Soon after we pass over Interstate 81, the Pennsylvania Farm Show Complex and Expo Center will be on the right.

Ed Kelemen

~IV~

HARRISBURG AND THE HEX HIGHWAY

The Pennsylvania State Lunatic Hospital

Near the Intersection of Maclay and Cameron Streets
Harrisburg

The Pennsylvania Farm Show and Expo Complex is located at 2300 North Cameron Street in Harrisburg. Maybe you have been there for one of the more than 200 shows and events scheduled each year, among them are gun shows, dance competitions, auto racing, pet expos, archery championships, bull riding, home-school association conventions, fire expos, collector car auctions, and professional soccer, just to name a few. Surely something on that schedule appeals to you. Of course, the annual Pennsylvania Farm Show in January gives the place its name.

If you are attending any of these great events, take a look across Cameron Street as you enter the parking complex. Hidden behind those beautiful oak trees on the hill overlooking the Farm Show Complex is the former Pennsylvania State Lunatic Asylum.

It was opened in 1851 as a result of the prodding of Dorothea Dix, an activist for social justice, including the humane treatment of what she called the indigent insane. Her herculean efforts created the first generation of asylums in the United States. The State Lunatic Hospital in Harrisburg was the first one of its kind in Pennsylvania. During the Civil War and for a time afterward, it did double duty as a convalescent hospital for soldiers.

Over the years the asylum grew beyond its founder's greatest dreams, eventually becoming known as the city on the Hill. It grew to more than 1,000 acres and over seventy buildings. It was self-sufficient. On the grounds were a farm, power plant, library, stores, and laundry, mostly staffed with patient labor. The place even had its own patient newspaper, *Heard on the Hill.*

The patient quarters were given such labels as Psychopathic, Convalescent, and Violent. The treatment of patients seems barbaric by today's standards, but it was cutting-edge at the time. Originally, treatment consisted of giving the patients plenty of fresh air, good food, and serene rest. This changed as the 1800s passed into the 1900s.

A new method of psychiatric care called hydrotherapy came into vogue and was popular for the next fifty years. The most common form of hydrotherapy was to wrap anxious or agitated patients tightly from head to toe in wet sheets and leave them lying on a table for extended periods of time. This was supposed to have a calming effect. Other forms of hydrotherapy included rain baths, fully submerged baths in large tubs, and forced colonic irrigation (enemas).

In 1921, the institution was renamed the Harrisburg State Hospital. In the 1930s surgical procedures to treat insanity, including lobotomies, were introduced, as were both electro and insulin shock therapy. In 1952 psychotropic drugs became the state-of-the-art treatment.

In 1921, the word "lunatic" was removed from the hospital's name and it was renamed "The Harrisburg State Hospital."

On January 27, 2006, the hospital closed its doors.

It is no wonder that after being populated for 156 years with traumatized mentally and physically ill patients, many of whom died on the premises, the facility is home to many haunts.

Since the asylum closed, the buildings have all been converted to other uses for various state agencies, including the Department of Agriculture and the General Services Administration. Staff and visitors report hearing disembodied screams, noises that have no explanation, and random footsteps echoing along walkways and throughout the historic buildings. Shadow figures frequently flit across people's field of vision, and apparitions presumed to be former patients walk the grounds and the hallways of the former hospital wards.

Staff and visitors report hearing disembodied screams, noises that have no easily understood explanation, and random footsteps echoing along walkways and throughout the historic buildings. Shadow figures frequently flit across people's field of vision, and apparitions of entities presumed to be former patients walk the grounds and the hallways of the former hospital wards.

The two areas where paranormal activity are most concentrated are in the basement: the warren of tunnels running beneath the complex and the former morgue, where blood-like stains appear on the floor of what was once the cadaver examining room. Cadaver examination must have been a messy process. During an investigation of the complex, the Harrisburg Area Paranormal Society captured a photo of a shadowy figure there.

The morgue was featured during the second season of the Discovery Channel series "Ghost Lab," in 2010. Investigators came away with several EVPs, including a spirit speaking the names "Peter" and "Annie."

If you visit this place, be forewarned: It is a hotbed of poltergeist activity. Watch out for independently moving and flying objects. If you're on a motorcycle, you're already prepared. Just leave your helmet on.

A couple of miles across the city is a mansion where a widow has been waiting for her husband's return for over two centuries. Continuing on Cameron Street, take a right onto Maclay Street and go as far as you can without getting wet in the river. At that point, turn right onto Front Street and ride along the riverbank. South Street will be on the left in a mile and a quarter, but since it's one-way the wrong way, you'll have to go around the block to get to our destination.

The Pennsylvania Bar Association (Formerly the Maclay Mansion)

100 South Drive
Harrisburg

Nearly two and a quarter centuries ago, Pennsylvania's first senator, William Maclay, built a mansion and moved into it with his wife, Mary Harris Maclay. Because of her husband's habit of keeping irregular hours, coming home at who knows what time of night, Mrs. Maclay would fret and worry about him. She would not retire for the evening until he arrived safely home. Until then, she paced the floors of the mansion, frequently peering out the windows in hope of catching a glimpse of him.

On April 16, 1804, he went away for the last time,

never to return to his beloved mansion. Instead he was laid to rest in Old Paxtang Cemetery some three and a half miles away. But his widow has never stopped watching for his return.

Even though the mansion has passed from the ownership of the Maclay family and is now the headquarters of the Pennsylvania Bar Association, Mary Maclay still roams the halls, rooms, and staircases, candelabra in hand, peering out the windows waiting for her husband. Employees have witnessed these activities and are often piqued at her habit of moving items around on their desks. One former executive director, Theodore Stellwag, was even prevented from entering an office one late night when she held the unlocked door closed. When he was finally able to wrench it open, he encountered an icy spot just over the threshold.

Take a good long look at the windows over the entrance. You just may see a spectral face slightly illuminated by candlelight peering back. But she won't be looking at you; she's watching for her husband's return.

If he hasn't shown up in over 200 years, he probably won't make an appearance while we're here, so let's leave for points east.

Head back down Front Street to Market Street, and turn left. A quarter mile along Market Street brings us to North Cameron, where we'll turn left again. After about a mile and a half, come to Interstate 81. Head north, then feed right onto Interstate 78 heading east. In 21 miles, Exit 13 will bring us to Bethel, the home of the Hex Highway, just one more name for Old Route 22.

Pennsylvania's Hex Highway
Berks County

Pennsylvania's Hex Highway shares the road with Old Route 22 from Bethel to Hamburg. Along this stretch of road you can see numerous barns and buildings decorated with the geometric circular designs known as hex signs. No, they are not intended to put a hex on anyone.

These designs are intended as protection against ill fortune and evil and bringers of good luck. They originally appeared on birth and marriage certificates, pottery, furniture, and clothing. In the mid-1800s, when exterior paint became more affordable, the Pennsylvania Dutch (actually Pennsylvania *Deutsch*, or German) settlers started putting the signs on their barns and houses.

A July 2006 article in the *New York Times* compared hex signs to ghosts, since they are fading from existence. It costs over $500 to repaint a hex sign on a barn. And most barns as they age are being replaced by less expensive metal ones, on which hex signs look out of place.

As you ride this stretch of Old Route 22 through the Pennsylvania Dutch country, watch for the hex signs on the barns. When you locate one, take a picture and treasure it. You have just caught a ghost of times past in your camera.

>*<

A little side trip off the main road along PA Route 419 South will get us heading in the direction of Womelsdorf, Pennsylvania. But before we get that far, let's make a left turn onto Charming Forge Road and check out the mansion at 274 Charming Forge Road.

Charming Forge Mansion

274 Charming Forge Road
Womelsdorf, Marion Township

A few miles south of Route 22 along PA Route 419 lies the town of Womelsdorf where Henry "Baron" Steigel built an iron-working operation around 1750 that he named "Charming Forge." George Ege was "Baron" Steigel's nephew and learned everything there was to know about operating an iron foundry and forge from him. Then in 1774, at the age of 26, George took over ownership and operation of Charming Forge.

He expanded the forge, using captured Hessian soldiers from the Revolutionary War and built a mansion that he named after the forge, becoming one of the county's wealthiest citizens.

George entered politics after the war and was elected

to the Pennsylvania House of Representatives in 1783, served as an associate judge in Berks County from 1791 until 1818 and also served as a member of the U.S. Congress from 1796 to 1797.

The mansion still sits along Charming Forge Road in Womelsdorf and is considered to be the "finest 'country' house in the early days of our nation."

Along with all this history, the mansion brings a couple of spirits to those who enter through its front doors made of the "finest Philadelphia woodwork."

During its heyday as the domicile of one of Pennsylvania's founding father's, a number of servants were employed to insure the smooth running of the mansion. After all, such a wealthy man as George Ege couldn't be bothered with the day-to-day minutiae of operating a house.

One of George's servants was a young lady employed as a kitchen maid. One day, while going about her daily chores, her voluminous skirts brushed too close to the open-hearth fire in the kitchen. They flashed into fire and consumed her before anyone could douse the flames. She still stays in the mansion and is seen from time-to-time hurrying along the hallways enroute to some unknown destination within the mansion. At least she isn't accompanied by the flames that consumed her.

Another spirit, this one of unknown origins haunts the mansion. It is of a man wearing a tri-corn hat of the type popular during the American Revolutionary times. He likes to hang out in one of the second floor bedrooms.

As if this isn't enough, the sound of the mansion's original owner, George Ege is heard when he enters by way of the back door as was his habit in life. He then clomps up the stairs to the second floor and becomes silent, possibly retiring for the night.

If you're interested in owning a haunted mansion of this kind, it was listed for sale a couple of years ago for the asking price of just a tad over one-and-a-third million dollars.

Oh well, dreams of the Lifestyles of the Rich and Famous. This neighborhood is a bit pricey for me. What say we head back north and travel east on the Hex Highway again? I don't know about you, but my wallet is haunted by the ghosts of dollars past.

Shartlesville Hotel

**Hex Highway
Shartlesville**

Speaking of ghosts along the Hex Highway, the Shartlesville Hotel is a mere shadow of its former self. It was built during the 19th century as a stagecoach stop and restaurant for dusty travelers en route to and from New York City and points west and east. It quickly became a favorite stop for them, and both it and the town prospered. President Franklin D. Roosevelt once stayed there. His visit was the subject of a feature article in *Collier's* magazine in 1950.

The hotel was a survivor, changing to meet the needs

of both its proprietors and its clients. To supplement the income from room rentals, it had at least one incarnation as a brothel. Our haunt stems from that time.

One of the ladies of the night who plied her trade at the hotel was a girl named Linda. One morning she was found hanging in a doorway of the hotel. She was quickly cut down but to no avail. She was dead. No one could figure whether she had been murdered or had committed suicide.

Her spirit remained, and she appeared to visitors, employees, and residents alike until the hotel shuttered its doors forever. But she didn't communicate with those who encountered her. Her death remained unsolved for over 100 years – until one night in 2010 when the Philadelphia Paranormal Society was called in to investigate. They located an extremely angry male entity, as well as the spirit of Linda sobbing inconsolably.

They learned that the man was a traveler who visited her frequently on his trips through the town. She had fallen in love with him, but this was his last visit. He was breaking off the relationship because he thought it might threaten his marriage. Yep, the cad was married.

Although not all the details of their encounter were revealed, the young lady was recorded as saying, "They killed me." The paranormal investigators deduced that she must have been murdered, then hanged in the doorway to make it appear to be suicide, leaving the perpetrator or perpetrators to be punished by karma alone. That ambiguous "They" casts doubt on her erstwhile lover acting alone. Maybe some silver changed hands. Who knows?

The death knell was rung for the hotel in 1995 when it was sold at a sheriff's sale. It is no longer either a hotel or a restaurant. Just like the seven gas stations that once lined Main Street, the Shartlesville Hotel has been bypassed by Interstate 78.

A little over six miles farther east on the Hex Highway brings us to the town of Hamburg on the Schuylkill River. Take a leisurely ride along the river as we contemplate our next pair of hauntings.

The Schuylkill River

Hamburg, PA

In 1779 an enterprising fellow by the name of Martin Kaercher divided a 250-acre land grant that he inherited from his father into building lots. Surprising enough, he named it after himself: Kaercher Stadt. The many German immigrants who purchased those lots were having none of that. In 1787, they named it after one of their hometowns in Germany, Hamburg.

Located along the Schuylkill River, on the path of the Centre Pike between Pottsville and Reading, on the Schuylkill Canal, and along a major railroad line, the town prospered and grew.

Today the hamlet is famous for two major festivals. On Saturday of Labor Day weekend is the Hamburg-er

Festival, which has grown each year since 2003. As its name implies, it is devoted to that famous sandwich, the hamburger. At last count it drew more than 30,000 visitors to more than 24 hamburger stands, three stages of continuous entertainment, and dozens and dozens of artisans and craft booths.

Hamburg's other festival has been around a bit longer. The King Frost Parade is billed as "the Largest Fall Extravaganza Parade on the East Coast." The first King Frost Parade happened in 1910. It took place from time to time for the next 54 years. It has been held every year since 1964 and attracted nearly 25,000 onlookers during the 2013 parade. Even though it takes place on the weekend closest to Halloween, it is not a Halloween parade. It is a celebration of Fall, welcoming King Frost as he ascends the throne for the winter months on the horizon.

If you are there for either festivals, notice the Schuylkill River running along the edge of town. Long before Germans or any other immigrants from across the Atlantic Ocean set foot on America's shores, the Native American tribe known as the Lenni Lenape roamed the wilderness and rivers of the area.

They spoke of supernatural beings that inhabit the Schuylkill River in the form of glowing lights. If you stand on the banks of that river after dark, and if it is quiet enough, you may be treated to a visit from those ancient spirits. Never fear; they will not approach nor harm you. They seem to be content to live in the brush on the bank of the river like wood sprites.

A couple of miles south of town is the Five Locks area of the Schuylkill Canal, which follows the river. Along the towpath you may see a girl strolling the path, or perhaps floating in the air above the canal. She usually appears at midnight during the full moon as a tenuous mist that coalesces into her shape. She seems to be searching for someone or something and will not communicate with you. Local folklore has it that she drowned in the canal, though nobody knows whether she jumped, fell, or was pushed.

Take a break and enjoy a meal at one of the many restaurants in and around Hamburg. While you're dining, think about our next stop, the location of what was probably Pennsylvania's first serial killer. When you are ready, head a bit north and get onto Interstate 78/U.S. 22, heading east again. Exit 35 will bring us to PA Route 143. Turn left onto PA 143 North and follow the signs to Hawk Mountain Bird Sanctuary. Perhaps the avian serenity will bring peace to this mountain, which has witnessed so many victims being sent to the Great Beyond before their scheduled times. It's just a few miles north of the Hex Highway.

Ghosts of Hawk Mountain

Hawk Mountain Bird Sanctuary
1700 Hawk Mountain Road
Kempton

The ride to the top of Hawk Mountain is along a beautiful two-lane, twisty road that offers scenic vistas interspersed with cathedral woods on every curve and straightaway. It's no wonder that the Lenni Lenape tribes revered the mountain.

Perhaps it was the majestic beauty of the mountain that brought the Gerhardt family to settle on its slope. They built a small cabin there and proceeded to live their dream, eking out an existence while increasing the size of their family. In 1756, as the French and Indian War reached fever pitch, the Lenni Lenape, urged on by the

French, massacred the entire family. Maybe the sacrilege of their trespass on sacred grounds was part of the motive for the raid. We'll never know.

One thing we do know is that there was one survivor of the massacre: 11-year-old Matthias Gerhardt. He was a determined, courageous young man who later returned to the family homestead, built a new home over the ashes of the original one, and lived out his days in defiance of the dangers of the mountain. His slain family often walked the area, the trees echoing with their death cries.

Years later another Matthias, this one with the last name Schambacher, opened a tavern and an inn at the old Gerhardt house. He and his wife didn't really seem suited to be innkeepers. They weren't outgoing, didn't like to associate with the local people, and pretty much kept to themselves.

Which was perfectly fine with the locals, who didn't like to visit the tavern anyway. Most people, locals and travelers alike, who spent a night at the tavern/inn swore they would never return. They said they could hear furtive footsteps that stopped outside their rooms and heavy breathing as though someone was eavesdropping. The barn was host to all sorts of strange sounds, wailing and screaming sounds came from the woods, and horses tried to bolt when being directed to the inn. Weird lights were often seen flashing through the trees as well. More than one traveler reported seeing Matthias Schambacher scrubbing what appeared to be blood from the barn walls.

That's because, for some of the travelers, the tavern was their *final* destination. Matthias plied them with alcohol to lessen their defenses and then murdered them. He confessed to this on his deathbed in the 1870s. He said that he dismembered his victims and toss some of the parts down a well. Other parts he scattered in the woods for scavengers to feast upon. He and his wife Margaret would then inventory the victims' belongings and sell them for personal gain.

He was observed in nearby Hamburg selling clothing and personal items from time to time. On at least one occasion a sutler stayed overnight at the Schambacher Inn and was never seen again. But shortly after his stay there, Matthias was in town selling Civil War uniforms and equipment identical to sutler's stock in trade.

Another visitor to the inn told locals that Schambacher tried to sell him some of his specialty, "old German sausage." Looking around the inn, the fellow saw no evidence of pigs or other livestock, so he politely declined.

Shambacher claimed that he didn't want to commit these heinous acts. He was forced to do so by "a great evil that lived on the mountain and whispered to him constantly, urging him to murder, even while he slept." Schambacher was buried in an unmarked grave at the New Bethel Church Cemetery. As his body was being lowered into the three-by-six grave, the gravediggers were scattered by a bolt of lightning that struck the blank headstone.

Tragedy at the inn didn't cease with Schambacher's death. It lay vacant for a few years. Then a third man by the name of Matthias took possession. He was a devout Catholic and reputed to be a holy man. He was known to be generous and kind, holding church services at the inn on Sundays for all comers, even baptizing some of the local children. The locals thought that the curse of the mountain had ended and it was once again the holy place revered by the Lenni Lenape.

They were wrong.

One summer day in 1890 day a hiker came to the inn. As he approached the building, he noticed that furniture, crockery, and other items were broken and scattered all over the yard. Next he found the front door had been forcibly ripped from its stout hinges. The building had been ransacked. Matthias, the holy man of the mountain, was missing.

A search party was quickly formed to search for him. A few days passed before his decapitated body was found discarded in the woods. The murderer was never identified, and poor Matthias's head was never found.

Afterward the building was the home to the Turner family, whose ten children seemed to chase the spirits of evil away with their exuberance for the twenty years that family occupied it. Then it was home to John Wenz, who used it as a gathering place where he and his friends could let down their hair without fear of disturbing the neighbors. That's because there were none. They even installed a still during Prohibition.

In 1938, the mountain was returned to the possession of nature when the Hawk Mountain Bird Sanctuary opened on nearly 1,400 acres that included its summit. The following year, John Lenz sold the old house to the sanctuary. It was renovated and has been the home of sanctuary staff and caretakers ever since.

The quiet solitude of the mountain since the founding of the sanctuary has been a benevolent environment for the spirits who call it home. They populate the slopes and summit with gleeful abandon.

A spirit described as a man ten feet tall appears along and sometimes in the middle of the narrow, convoluted two-lane Hawk Mountain Road, startling drivers.

Thankfully, no accidents have been attributed to his appearance. Yet. Sometimes he appears to birdwatchers along the Kittatinny Ridge, scaring the bejeebers out of them. People say that he emanates pure evil, bringing terror to even the stoutest hearts. More likely he is donning that cloak of malevolence to keep trespassers away from his sacred resting place. He is probably the oldest haunt of the hill, thought to be one of the spirits of the Indian burial grounds disturbed by the first European settlers.

Ever since the old inn has been inhabited by sanctuary personnel, strange things have happened around it. Mysterious faces appear at the windows. Horrible screams of anguish are heard at odd times during the nights. Are they echoes of travelers being brutally murdered? Or are they the death cries of the massacred Gerhardt family being scalped alive?

Occasionally the remains of one of Schambacher's victims are unearthed in the surrounding woods. Might those screams at night be directing people to the locations of the corpses?

The shades of a little German-speaking girl and her parents haunt the house. They are often heard conversing in Deutsch. The little girl is usually seen hovering about a foot and a half off the floor (the exact distance the floor was lowered during renovations). She is the ghost of a child who fell down the stairs of the building, breaking her neck. On rare occasions she plays her little penny whistle to entertain the occupants.

A ruined shack on the ridge was the home of a witch. People who come upon it experience her noisy displeasure at being disturbed, even though she has been dead for many decades.

Retracing our path will bring us back down the mountain to Route 22, where we will head on east until Exit 49. The Allentown suburb of Alburtis is about eight miles south of U.S. 22 from this exit. There we will stop at a restaurant that includes ghosts on the menu.

The Maple Grove Inn

2165 State Street
Alburtis

There aren't many eating establishments that tell you right on their menu that a haunt may join you during your dinner. The Maple Grove Inn is the only one I know. The inn has a long and varied history, with its main constant the quality of its food. And its haunts.

It opened its door in 1783 after John Keifer built it as a place for the suppliers of his many gristmills to stay and sup. As traffic in the area increased, it evolved into a stagecoach stop where travelers could stay overnight and enjoy fine vittles.

During its early years, an area woman became enamored of a member of one of the local Indian tribes. Her secret affair with Charlie, as he was known, ran its course as those things do, and she became pregnant. When it became obvious that she was with child and the father was identified, the people of the town could not believe that she had fallen in love with a savage. It had to be rape. So Charlie was unceremoniously dragged into the Common Room of the inn by a group of outraged citizens and hanged from one of the rafters in front of the fireplace. Before he died, he vowed to forever haunt the inn. There is no mention of whether alcohol was involved in the proceedings, but I have my suspicions.

Charlie is still unsatisfied upset by the injustice of it all, and he makes his feelings known. When the fireplace is lighted, it wakes up his spirit and he starts his demonstration. His footsteps resound throughout the room. He rattles the fireplace tools and causes the chandeliers to tremble and swing. Not satisfied with that, he plays with light switches, locks and unlocks doors, raps on the walls, and whistles, providing ethereal entertainment to all who watch and listen. Sometimes he actually appears, taking the form of a mist or a dove. Legend has it that his earthly remains lie under the hearth of the fireplace – or possibly in the basement of the building. His exact location has been lost over time.

Charlie isn't the only ghost who has decided that the accommodations at the Maple Grove Inn are to his liking. Another fellow who lost his life there prematurely has stayed on. He was found murdered in one of the upstairs closets. Not quite a rambunctious as Charlie, this one confines himself to noisy footsteps when there is no one else around.

The innkeepers will tell you, "Charlie, our resident ghost, is a friend to all who stop at the Inn and would like to guide you and your guests through an enjoyable and unforgettable evening filled with fine spirits and culinary delights." This is one place where "fine spirits" don't confine themselves to glasses and bottles.

After a sumptuous dining experience at this historic restaurant, we'll let our food settle as we wend our way back the few miles to Interstate 78/U.S. 22 and head east again. Where U.S. 22 peels off the Interstate, continue on 22 until the exit for PA 309. Take PA 309 North a couple of miles to the little town of Orefield, where a jilted Yankee girl still waits for her Confederate lover.

Magnolia's Vineyard

2204 Village Road
Orefield

This beautiful long frame building was built as the Guthsville Hotel during the 1850s. It served both locals and transients and was a very popular place, being located at a busy crossroads. Less than a dozen years after it opened, the Civil War struck, and it was a way station for many soldiers traveling to and from Camp Curtin in Harrisburg. Business was booming.

As the war progressed, the hotel was also used as a combination hospital, treatment center, and convalescent home for wounded soldiers.

One of those soldiers was a Union officer named Evans. Local lore has it that he was a general, but no record of a Union general named Evans can be found. Be that as it may, Officer Evans was accompanied by his daughter, Magnolia. When he had sufficiently recuperated to return to his unit, Magnolia stayed on to tend the other wounded soldiers. More were arriving daily.

One morning, a wounded Confederate soldier was brought to the hotel cum hospital. Magnolia took a special interest in the young Rebel and showered him with tender loving care (emphasis on the "loving"). She confessed her love for him and he reciprocated, promising everlasting love for her. When he had recovered enough to be paroled back to the South, the lovebirds were separated, but only until the end of the war. He swore to her that, as soon as the hostilities came to an end, he would return to claim his love, marry her, and take her home with him.

Well, April 1865 came and went. The Confederates had surrendered at Appomattox Courthouse in Virginia, but no ex-soldier appeared in Orefield to sweep his lady love off her feet. Months and years passed. She waited. The Guthsville Hotel was renamed Magnolia's Vineyard in honor of her faith in eternal love. He never returned. Did he perhaps die in one of the battles of the waning war? Nobody knows. But Magnolia waited.

She still waits for her soldier boy. If you go down by the banks of the Jordan Creek behind Magnolia's Vineyard on a misty summer evening, you may see her waiting still.

>*<

Our way back will take us by Dorney Park, one of the nation's premier amusement parks. Never fear, we'll be stopping there later. Just west of Dorney Park on U.S. Route 222 is what I consider a non-haunting, even though local lore says otherwise. You can stop by at your own discretion. Just after U.S. 222 passes Interstate 476, you will come to North Krocks Road on the right. A hundred or so feet up that road is the entrance to Resurrection Cemetery

~V~

Allentown

and the

Lehigh Valley

Resurrection Cemetery

547 Krocks Road
Allentown

I'm not too sure about this one. Though I've heard it told time and again, I can't track down any definitive information about the haunt. But, for what it's worth, I'm putting it here for your consideration.

Resurrection Cemetery in Allentown isn't all that old as cemeteries go, having been founded in 1968 by the Catholic Diocese of Allentown. So it doesn't share a multigenerational history with other haunted places in the area. Yet there is one haunt associated with it.

Local lore has it that a young lady who lived across Krocks Road from the location of the cemetery lost her life to tuberculosis during the 1940s and was subsequently buried in the cemetery in her favorite party gown. Since that time, many motorists in the area claim to have picked up a girl in a gown so white it glows. She says that she is lost and would appreciate a ride home to an address along Krocks Road. Then, as the car passes Resurrection Cemetery, she disappears.

Along with a number of other people, I feel that this is a case of mistaken identity. Except in this instance, the mistaken identity is the cemetery, not the spirit. There is another cemetery with the same name and the same story that predates this one by decades. It just so happens to have the same name as the final resting place of Resurrection Mary, who has been called Chicago's most famous ghost. Resurrection Mary solicits rides from folk driving along Archer Avenue in Willow Springs, Illinois, and has done so since 1939. As they ride along, Archer Avenue becomes Archer Road and passes Resurrection Cemetery on their right. And she disappears from the car, just as she has done for the last three-quarters of a century.

I think it's a case of right spirit, wrong cemetery. But let me know if you give her a ride.

Time for some recreation. Just on the other side of U.S. 222 lies Dorney Park, a place full of chills and thrills for the enthusiastic roller coaster and thrill-ride fan. For the rest of us, there are chills aplenty when the haunts join in the fun. Stop by, enjoy the rides, maybe get wet at Wildwater Kingdom, and have some crab fries.

Dorney Park

3830 Dorney Park Rd.
Allentown

Dorney Park is a great, world-famous amusement park. Rides like Demon Drop, Dominator, Stinger, Possessed, Monster, and Talon are enough to get most people's hearts pounding with chills, thrills, and downright terror. If they don't do it for you, a couple of haunts may do the trick.

It wasn't always that way. Solomon Dorney purchased the land where the park stands in 1860. That's when he built a fish hatchery there. Realizing that people need some diversion in their life, he also started a summer resort on that same property. It was a favored isle of tranquility for people to catch their breath and sanity during the Civil War. Over the next 20 years he added carnival games, a petting zoo, and playground facilities. These increased the resort's popularity, so Dorney built a hotel with a restaurant to serve the numerous visitors. In 1884, he named the enterprise Dorney's Trout Ponds and Summer Resort, and it has borne his name ever since.

During the next 100 years, the park expanded, changed hands a few times, and garnered international fame as the world-class amusement park it is today.

One of the park's most famous rides endured through a number of incarnations. During the early 1930s a dark ride named the Devil's Cave was built to titillate and startle the less hardy souls who rode it. Its most famous feature was Laffing Sal, an extremely plus-size woman who jiggled when she giggled and wiggled when she let go with her infectious guffaws. The Devil's Cave entertained generations of park attendees until 1963.

That year it was re-themed as the Pirate's Cove. Laffing Sal was reincarnated as a pirate complete with an eye-patch, a cutlass, and a buccaneer's chapeau. That lasted for 11 years until the ride was rebuilt again as the wildly popular Bucket of Blood. Then, nine short years later in 1983, a disastrous fire roared through the park and the Bucket of Blood burned to the ground.

With a history like this, you might assume that this is the haunted ride. Not so. That distinction goes to a lesser-known attraction called the Old Gold Mine ride. Built in 1970, it actually ran under the mansion that Solomon Dorney had called home. The yells and screams of the riders, along with the noise from the cars and sound effects of the ride from park opening until late at night, were just too much for the founder's spirit. He made his displeasure known by haunting both the ride and the old building until it was demolished.

The thrill ride known as the Dominator either blasts people to a height of 170 feet before dropping them back to earth or slowly lifts them to that same height, then slams them back to earth at speeds that defeat gravity. Near the Dominator is a building that houses the Edge, a gift shop. In one of the utility corridors between this building and another, employees are startled by a fellow who pops into existence and just as quickly disappears. Conjecture has it that he may be the spirit of old Solomon Dorney, who was displaced by the demolition of his home.

In 1917 a master carver, Daniel Muller, created horses for a carousel that was to travel the country in carnivals, circuses, and fairs for the next five decades. His wife absolutely fell in love with one of the masterpieces he created. In 1971 the carousel found a home at Cedar Point Amusement Park in Sandusky, Ohio. The grand old lady of the midway became a centerpiece in the Frontiertown area of the park. Shortly thereafter, Mrs. Muller's ghost found her beloved charger on the bank of Lake Erie and took it for a ride. As a matter of fact, she took it for many rides. The great old merry-go-round started up at all times of the night after Cedar Point had closed, complete with the whirring of the propulsive machinery, flashing lights, and the cacophony of carnival music booming from within. As the horses sped by, only one was occupied – by a gracious lady in white, laughing in glee as she rode her favorite steed.

In 1995, the carousel was sold to Dorney Park, but

Mrs. Muller's horse wasn't part of the deal. Today it is on display in Frontiertown at Cedar Point. Since she can no longer ride it in all its glory, some people think Mrs. Muller's spirit came to Dorney Park with Cedar Point's carousel. Park employees report that the antique ride now starts up from time to time during the night with no earthly influence. Although Mrs. Muller has not been seen, she may still be enjoying a ride on the merry-go-round that once held her wonderful stallion.

After a day of rides, cotton candy, popcorn, hot dogs, and of course crab fries, you may be too tired to do much more. But, if you have a reserve of energy, take a left out of Dorney Park and head east on Route 222, which is also known as Hamilton Boulevard. Six blocks along and we're at the intersection with South Cedar Crest Boulevard. Here is a 250-year-old historic haunted building that just may be gone by the time you read this.

King George Inn

**3141 Hamilton Blvd.
Dorneyville section of Allentown**

A bevy of ghosts are about to be permanently evicted from one of Allentown's oldest buildings. The King George Inn, built in 1756 and designated a National Historic Site by the National Park Service in 1976, is going to be demolished. Why? To make way for yet another shopping center complete with a bank, a motel, and a chain drugstore. Just what the town needs.

True, the inn has seen better days, but it has led a storied life. And it isn't its fault that it was named after Britain's King George III, the worst tyrant in our country's history and the impetus for the American Revolution.

In 1756, the King George Inn was built at a crossroads as a way station for travelers. Its stout stone walls also offered refuge and protection from marauding Native Americans during the French and Indian War.

During the American Revolution, General George Washington's troops bivouacked in the adjacent fields, conducting drills, while the officers headquartered at the inn.

Later on it served as a courthouse, town hall, and public meeting place. As a restaurant and tavern, it had several incarnations, being festooned with the names White Horse Inn and Ernie's Place before reverting to its original name during the late 1960s, when it was restored and reopened by local restaurateur Cliff McDermott.

Now it seems that time has passed it by. Fewer people dine at elegant historical restaurants when they can grab a quick bite at a fast-food place. When the King George Inn goes, it will leave behind a number of spirits that have called it home for the last two and a half centuries.

A woman and child of the French and Indian War era roam the old building dressed in attire of their time, appearing and fading from sight most often in the original basement. Sharing that space with them (but not at the same time) is a Revolutionary War soldier in full uniform, ready to meet the redcoats approaching Philadelphia.

A wailing baby is heard in the place where a well once supplied water for the inn. It is thought to be the ghost of an infant tossed into the well by attacking Native Americans during the French and Indian War to foul the water and bring the inhabitants out into the open, where they could be slaughtered.

Footsteps resound on the old wooden floors and steps when nobody is in the building, and a bearded visage appears throughout the building, surprising guests and staff alike.

And finally, there is Charlie, the mischievous spirit of a man who reportedly committed suicide by hanging himself during a stay at the inn. He busies himself by aggravating the kitchen staff, moving utensils and supplies and making them difficult to find when needed. He also happily startles people by slamming doors.

What is to become of these otherworldly inhabitants when this fine old historic building is no more (possibly by the time you read this)? Will Charlie amuse himself by disrupting operations behind the counter of a yet-to-be-built pharmacy? Will the woman and her child from the French and Indian War be mistaken for an ethereal housekeeper and child at a new chain motel? Will people assume that the fellow in Revolutionary War garb is a re-enactor? Will the front desk at that as-yet-unnamed motel be plagued with complaints about a crying baby?

I guess we'll just have to wait and see.

In the meantime, let's head north on Cedar Crest Boulevard. Pass through the intersection with Hamilton Boulevard Bypass, and the next street on the right will be the entrance to Cedar Crest College.

Cedar Crest College

100 College Drive
Allentown

Sitting on 84 acres in a beautiful suburban setting is this gem of an educational institution, which year after year is listed as one of the best liberal arts colleges in the country. Cedar Crest College was founded shortly after the Civil War, in 1867, as a private all-women school. Since then, the rules have been relaxed somewhat. Male students are now permitted to attend evening classes. Even so, out of a total enrollment of nearly 1,400 students, men account for less than 100.

Back in the middle of the 20th century there were no men on campus. However, youngsters are resourceful, and love always finds a way. One coed named Wanda somehow found her true love while attending the college. As has happened countless times throughout history, that love bore fruit and the lass found out that she was with child.

Unwed motherhood was an extreme social stigma during that time and was accompanied by nearly unbearable shame. Facing abandonment by her family and ostracism by society, poor Wanda saw no way out of her dilemma. Except one.

Taking a length of rope with her into the rear stairwell of her dormitory, Butz Hall, she tied a noose around her neck, secured the other end of the line to a banister, and dropped to her death.

But even in death, she felt that she wasn't welcome to return to her family, so she has lingered on in Butz Hall, wandering the hallways of that building. Students and staff alike encounter her as she roams the building.

Another spirit manifests herself in Butz Hall. The image of a young girl appears in a mirror in the laundry room. It has been seen in student rooms as well. Is it possible that little girl is Wanda's love child, who never had the opportunity to even be born?

It's something to take into account as we head for another of Allentown's famous institutes of higher learning. Head north on South Cedar Crest Boulevard, which becomes North Cedar Crest Boulevard as we cross Parkway Boulevard.. Take a right onto West Chew Street. In about a mile, we'll find ourselves in the middle of Muhlenberg College campus.

Muhlenberg College

2400 West Chew Street
Allentown

With a campus of gently winding roads, Muhlenberg College offers a serene, bucolic setting for its 2,500 students in the city of Allentown. It was founded in 1848 as a seminary for the Lutheran religion by the Reverend Samuel K. Brobst, a Reformed Lutheran Minister. In 1867, it was renamed after Henry Melchior Muhlenberg, the patriarch of the Lutheran Church in America. In 1905 the college moved to its present site in the western area of Allentown.

One of the college's early administrators was Oscar Bernheim, who served as a registrar or treasurer. He built his home in the southern part of the campus. His home gardens were his pride and joy. He loved puttering about in them and making them a showpiece. It was his way of relaxing at the end of a day or a week in the school's offices. Oscar loved the college as well, so much so that upon his death, he bequeathed his entire estate to Muhlenberg College. With one proviso: that his beloved garden be tended for perpetuity. For years his wishes were honored. And Oscar was a happy camper, even making a personal appearance from time to time in that garden. He would be seen tending to some of the less fortunate plants to bring them back to health. At other times he appeared in the hallways of his home and in the upstairs bedroom where he had expired.

Then came that fateful day when his wishes were trampled, along with his garden. The space where those plants grew was just too valuable to waste on plants. It was needed for the construction of new student housing, including South Hall. The conditions of Oscar's bequest were forgotten.

Oscar Bernheim makes his displeasure at the wanton destruction of his garden known in no uncertain terms. He moves things around at random in students; rooms and turns their televisions on and off in no particular pattern. These actions are relative innocuous, but other activities of a paranormal nature have been so disquieting for students that they have reported them to college administrators. Even a blessing by members of the Lutheran clergy has had no effect.

One talisman, however, has been found to assuage Oscar's ire. Students who keep a healthy growing plant in their room are not affected by the hauntings.

>*<

Continuing on through the campus will bring us to 19th Street. Turn right In a couple of blocks we'll turn left onto Hamilton Street, which also happens to be U.S. Route 222. If you're driving this way after dark, watch out for a staggering young lady. She seems to be destined to spend eternity here.

The Hamilton Street Ghost

Allentown

A half century ago, a young lady was hurrying home along Hamilton Street. Maybe she was late for supper, maybe inclement weather gave added impetus to her steps. For whatever reason she wasn't completely aware of her surroundings. She crossed the street by the old Hess Brothers Department Store. Another person was hurrying to a destination along Hamilton Street, except in a car. Maybe that person was late for supper. Maybe the windshield wasn't being cleared by worn wipers. It's all conjecture on my part.

The fates decreed that the two would meet violently and that young lady's life was ended at that intersection. Fifty some years later, the department store has been razed and replaced by the Pennsylvania Power and Light Plaza, but the spirit of that young lady still treads her fateful path of doom.

Drivers and pedestrians alike see her hurrying along the sidewalk with a dazed look on her face. Contrary to observers conclusions, she is neither drunk nor drugged. In fact she isn't even there. That becomes obvious when she turns to dart across the street and disappears before stepping off the sidewalk. Her spirit is trapped in an endless loop, possibly not even knowing that she has been dead for over 50 years.

Constitution Drive

Allentown

Not the easiest place to find, Constitution Drive parallels the railroad tracks for a ways along the Lehigh River. It is a decrepit two-lane road, barely paved and potholed, in an isolated area that has been traditionally used as a garbage dump. A feeling of malevolence pervades the area. Add the high crime rate – burglaries, shootings, arsons, and rapes – and it definitely isn't somewhere you want to be found alone. Plus, if the local police find you there, you may be in for a difficult time.

As if that cautionary note weren't enough, the road is haunted. The origin of the haunt is the subject of some speculation. It seems as though a guy was walking his two dogs along the railroad tracks next to the road one day when he was struck by a passing train and killed. The train amputated one of his legs in the process. That much, all the stories agree upon. However, one version has him slowly dying over a period of days alongside the desolate road, his dogs at his side guarding him. Another has him and his dogs being killed instantly, while yet another tells how the dogs refused to leave the spot where he died and finally starved to death on the spot.

No matter which version is right, he walks his dogs along the road to this day, his crimson glowing eyes giving away his sepulchral essence. Sometimes after a winter storm two sets of dog tracks are left imprinted in the snow, but only one human footprint between them is visible.

I hate to leave such a nice city on a somber note, but our next stop is in Northampton, Pennsylvania. We will be heading north on 17th Street, which becomes PA Route 145 and takes us four miles to PA Route 329. There we will turn right, cross the Lehigh River, and then turn left onto Main Street in Northampton. We will find the Roxy Theater about to celebrate its centennial with a house full of ghosts at the birthday party.

The Roxy Theater

2004 Main Street
Northampton

Take a look above the brightly lighted marquee of the Roxy Theater and you will see the word "Lyric" chiseled into the granite capstone of the building. That's because the theater was originally called the Lyric by builder Harry Hartman when he opened its doors to the public during the winter of 1921. Twelve years later, hard hit by the Great Depression, the Lyric closed its doors. It was sold to a group from Philadelphia who renovated and reopened it as the Roxy. And, that's been its name ever since as it hosted such acts as Bruce Springsteen, Billy Joel, Blood Sweat and Tears, and Kiss. Its stage has seen many theatrical productions along with its mainstay, movies.

The Roxy is such a wonderful venue, reminiscent of

the great theaters of the 1930s and '40s, that it's no surprise that remnants of theatergoers of yesteryear have remained. Murmurings of a restless audience down in the lower level can be heard when nobody can be seen. It's as though they are patiently waiting for the curtains to open for another show. Speaking of those curtains, they have been known to move with no earthly assistance, as though spectral actors are maneuvering backstage for an opening night. Maybe to lend a little melodic support to those phantom actors, that great seven-rank Wurlitzer organ starts up on its own, even when it isn't plugged in.

And, should you decide to stay for one of the live shows or movies, leave room in the back row of the lower level for the dark shadow man who moves from seat to seat, looking for the one with the best view. He must be a really picky person, because all the seats in the Roxy are good ones.

>*<

Next we will visit another institution of higher learning, Lehigh University in Bethlehem. Directions from Northampton seem straightforward, but following them will be tricky. Get back on PA Route 329. Follow it until we come to Weaverville Road, about a mile and a half. Turn right onto Weaverville Road and follow its curves and twists until Airport Road (which is also PA Route 987). Turn right and stay on 987 until we get to U.S. Route 22. Follow 22 east for one exit, then head south on PA Route 378 (which also goes by the name of Fred B. Rooney Highway). Follow Route 378 until you see Lehigh University on the hill in front of you. Stop in and say hi to the cranky old ghost who haunts the university's library.

Linderman Library

Lehigh University
Library Drive
Bethlehem

In 1865 Asa Packer, a wealthy local businessman, donated $500,000 plus the land to begin Lehigh University as an engineering school blended with traditional university studies. That half-million dollar endowment was the single largest gift ever received by a university up to that time. In fact, that gift was so generous that no student was required to pay tuition until 1891. Admission was based on a competitive exam.

Grateful educators and associates of Mr. Parker exhorted him to name the university after himself. But he demurred, instead naming it after the Lehigh Valley

Railroad, which he both loved and controlled.

Since then the school has doubled in size many times over. Today the university numbers nearly 7,500 students. The original 60 acres of land donated by patriarch Asa Parker sits in the northern corner of the university's 2,350 acres.

Nestled within the university's original complex is beautiful Linderman Library, an example of the late 1800's most beautiful architecture. Soaring towers and crenelated turrets top off the exterior of this cathedral-appearing structure. Huge windows bring light within to the generations of scholars who have laboriously pored over countless tomes in the last 125-plus years. The interior is bathed in soft light from the unbelievable stained-glass artwork that acts as both a skylight and a dome for the main part of the building.

The building may be old, and it may be steeped in history, tradition, and artistry. But it has kept up with the times. It is a state-of-the-art university college research facility, with all the bells and whistles of the computer age.

With Lucy's Cafe within, it's small wonder that the library is a favored place to meet friends, grab a cup of coffee, and catch up on the latest news.

That brings us to possibly the library's most famous patron. Many years ago, so many in fact that nobody can recall his name, an elderly gentleman frequented the library. I guess the main reason that no one remembered his name is because he was such a pain in the posterior that they actively tried to forget him when he wasn't there. However, while he was present he was always treated with deference and the politeness that has been the hallmark of the school. The cantankerous old curmudgeon felt so at home within the walls of Linderman Library that he stayed on even after his corporeal self departed this world.

Students and staff alike have been pestered by the old fellow, who has made a longer than lifetime career of being a general nuisance. Luckily, it is rare that a customer gets elbowed by the old crank while sipping a cup of coffee or tea.

Within walking distance is Fourth street, with a myriad of shops and cafes to entice you. While strolling along, take a gander at 114 West Fourth Street. Read on to find out what happens when you open a restaurant over people's last stop before the graveyard.

Anna Mia's Restaurant

**114 West 4th Street
Bethlehem**

There are some places where you just shouldn't build. People have learned this lesson the hard way over the years. Don't build over Native American sacred grounds; nothing good will come of it. Remember the people who tried to inhabit Hawk Mountain (a mere 40 miles to the west)? Don't move a cemetery and build on that ground. The previous inhabitants might not like it. Just ask the patrons at the Lawrenceville branch of the Carnegie Library in Pittsburgh.

Now there's another one to add to the list. And it should have been a no-brainer. Unless you want unwelcome guests annoying your customers and staff, don't put a restaurant in a building that formerly housed a funeral parlor.

The owners of Anna Mia's Restaurant didn't consider that when they opened a fine Italian eatery at the location of the former Cantelmi's Funeral Home. From the day they opened, they were treated to phantom footsteps and voices coming from places that were not occupied by a living person. Strange music emanated from within the building, but it could not be traced to a source. Wall hangings crashed to the floor for no apparent reason, startling everyone nearby.

The owners pooh-poohed the events and said that they weren't concerned. They were of the opinion that the haunt was a friendly spirit and added some spice to the ambiance. The spirit's camaraderie notwithstanding, Anna Mia's is no more, and passersby are no longer treated to the aroma of marinara sauce wafting on the air in the middle of this block.

Let's keep heading west on Fourth Street until we come to Wyandotte Street. Take a right onto Wyandotte and cross the Lehigh River heading north. On the other side of the river, take the ramp for Main Street. Our first stop will be at the oldest continuously-operated bookstore in the whole wide world.

The Moravian Book Shop

**428 Main Street
Bethlehem**

The oldest continuously operated book shop in the world is located on Main Street in Bethlehem, Pennsylvania. It was founded in 1745 by the Moravian Church, and today it helps to support the Moravian Ministerial Fund. From the time when the first operator, Samuel Powell, opened the bookstore on the south bank of the Lehigh River, it moved several times before settling into its present location in 1871.

Boasting a comprehensive collection of Moravian, Bethlehem, and Lehigh Valley books, it also has a vast collection of other books for sale and can ship just about any book in print to any address. That's not all. The bookstore is also an outlet for Christmas and Bethlehem-themed gifts, especially stars of all types. When you visit, be sure to pick up some tins of delicious Moravian cookies made from a 200 year-old recipe.

One reason the bookstore has survived for well over 250 years just may be its guardian ghost. A specter has been roaming the aisles and poking into the building's nooks and crannies as long as anyone can remember.

He is described as a man dressed in a long coat or a robe of some sort. He has been seen by many people, employees and customers alike. Occasionally a book will "fall" from a shelf seemingly at random. Staff members know not to replace it on the shelf. Nope, they keep it close by the cash register. That's because inevitably someone will be in later in the day to purchase that very same book. The ghost is saving the staff the trouble of looking for the book for that customer.

One time the ghost saved the shop from a calamity. Staff members saw him running through the store toward the kitchen area one evening as though he was agitated. They followed him and found that the burners had been left ignited in the oven. The oven was shut off, averting a catastrophe, and the guardian ghost was thanked for his help.

As you exit the bookshop, look across the street and you will see the huge, historic Hotel Bethlehem.

Historic Hotel Bethlehem
437 Main Street

Bethlehem

Across the street from the Moravian Book Shop sits the majestic Hotel Bethlehem. Its spectral residents aren't quite as helpful as the one at the bookstore, but they are quite entertaining nevertheless.

In 1741, Moravian missionaries built on the site of today's hotel the "First House of Bethlehem." At the time, that solitary building sat on the bank of a fresh running stream in the middle of the wilderness. On December 24 of that year, Christmas Eve, Count Nicholas Von Zinzendorf, a Moravian patron traveling under the name of Domine de Thuirstein, sang a hymn about Bethlehem, and the decision was made to name the little settlement after the location of Christ's birth.

In 1794, the Golden Eagle Hotel was erected on that spot. It served tourists and business travelers for the next century and a quarter before coming to the end of its days as a convalescent home for wounded soldiers returning home from World War I. The Golden Eagle Hotel closed its doors in April of 1919.

Three years later, after an infusion of $800,000 from steel magnate Charles M. Schwab and other Bethlehem businessmen, the world-class historic Bethlehem Hotel opened its doors. It immediately became *the* place to stay in eastern Pennsylvania. It was host to five Presidents of the United States, Winston Churchill, the Prime Minister of Great Britain, the Dalai Lama, and countless A-list entertainers and sports figures.

During Prohibition, the hotel boasted a hidden speakeasy. For a while, it sold its own brand of cigars. The tile on the floor in the fabulous 1741 on the Terrace Dining Room was made at the Moravian Tile Works in Doylestown. It is the same Moravian tile found in Pennsylvania's Capitol building in Harrisburg, as well as in the world-famous Monte Carlo Casino in Monte Carlo.

The hotel changed hands after 1960 and fell on hard times for a short while before being brought back to its original splendor and elegance by Robert and Dee Decker, Bethlehem developers who purchased it in 1984.

With all this history it would be unconscionable for the stately building to be without ghosts. Not to disappoint anyone, it is filled to the rafters with spirits of all types, mostly benign. It is commonplace for both visitors and staff to encounter shadows that fade as quickly as they appear, see transparent figures roaming the halls and stairwells, or hear the elevator operated by an unseen being. The cold spots cannot be attributed to anomalies in the state-of-the-art heating system, and you just may feel a tap on the shoulder or hear your name called when you think you are alone.

And that's just the anonymous spirits roaming about. A raft of colorful people who enjoyed their stays at the hotel so much that their spirits decided to stay on are well known.

One has been identified as Francis "Daddy" Thomas, a devout Moravian who was famous for his fearlessness in the face of danger. In his younger days, around the 1750s, he was a courier, delivering mail and dispatches through the Indian-controlled area. At that time, couriers faced several dangers – not only roaming Indian bands but also marauding thieves, since they were often known to carry valuables. Once Daddy was thrown from his horse so severely that he fractured his neck and was carried home on a litter, assumed to be dead. But he escaped the Reaper that time and recovered. Another time he plunged through thick ice on horseback into frigid waters, exposing himself to the dual dangers of drowning and exposure. Once again, he cheated Death and recovered.

Daddy Thomas eventually gave up his life of danger and became a cabinetmaker, married, and settled down. Although he and his wife had no children of their own during their 53-year marriage, they raised three children of Moravian missionaries. All three were sent to study at the famous Moravian Girls' Seminary at Bethlehem.

During all those years, Daddy was Bethlehem unofficial ambassador, welcoming everyone who visited the town. He became famous for his kindness and upbeat disposition and was a favorite of townspeople and travelers as well.

After his death in 1822, Daddy Thomas stayed on to watch over and welcome people to the place he loved so much when he was alive.

Wearing his black tricorn hat and a long, black woolen cape, he has been spotted in the boiler room of the hotel near a filled-in escape tunnel used by the Moravians to avoid capture during Indian raids. He once appeared to a night engineer before disappearing in a puff of smoke that traveled across the boiler room. That engineer took to locking himself in his office and observed shadows moving on the floor through the space at the bottom of the locked door. He need not have worried about any harmful intentions on the part of Daddy Thomas, who just seems to be concerned with the welfare of guests, especially female, who check in at the hotel.

Two other colorful ghosts are a married couple, the Brongs. In 1833, after serving as managers of the hotel for a short six months, they were asked to leave by a committee of the Moravian Church, owner of the hotel at that time. The churchmen were less than appreciative of the Brongs' intemperate habits.

Mr. Brong had the habit of joining nearly every hotel guest to help them slake their thirst and wash the dust from their throats. So much so that the bartender routinely had to just about carry Mr. Brong to a nearby bench when he could no longer stand unassisted.

While Mr. Brong was offending hotel guests with his frequent intoxication, Mrs. Brong was equally offensive to early 19th-century sensibilities in her own way. She had the scandalous habit of walking about barefoot – as one guest put it, with her "pedal extremities completely exposed."

The Brongs left the hotel at the request of the church committeemen, but Mrs. Brong wasn't that easy to get quit of. Although the exact date of her demise isn't a matter of record, she came back to spend her afterlife at the hotel where she was once asked to leave.

Mrs. Brong is often seen in the kitchen and dining areas of the Hotel Bethlehem, wearing clothing appropriate to her era, with one exception that pretty much identifies her: the apparition lacks both shoes and stockings. You might say that her pedal extremities are completely exposed.

Mary Augusta Yohe, called "May" by one and all, was born at the Eagle Hotel in April 1866. Her grandfather, Caleb Yohe, was then the popular innkeeper. May was blessed with a beautiful voice and a talent for dancing. She often entertained hotel guests in the lobby. Her talent was so obvious and beguiling that the Moravians took up a collection and sent her to Paris for formal operatic training.

Twenty years later she was recognized as one of the country's biggest stars, and her personal appearances always caused a sensation. She was the headliner wherever she went. Unfortunately, her rapid rise to stardom had an effect that we often seen today on young people thrust into celebrity before they achieve personal maturity. Her fame deteriorated into notoriety as her many flings became gossip fodder for the masses.

During the 1890s, May went to England for a command performance for Queen Victoria's son, Prince Edward, who adored her beautiful singing. While there, she met Lord Francis Clinton Hope, who owned the famous Hope diamond. She married him in short order. May was known to wear the diamond on certain occasions, despite the famous curse on it. Since its supposed theft from the forehead of an Indian idol in 1642, bad luck and death have been levied upon all who own or even touch it.

Whether the curse is true or not, Lord Hope was forced to sell the diamond in 1899 due to impending bankruptcy. May left him for the arms of a handsome American soldier the following year. May's choice was an unfortunate one, as the soldier stole all her jewelry and left her in the lurch. They reconciled, but then they broke up again, divorcing in 1905.

May's escapades damaged her popularity. She tried many comebacks, with limited success. Along with her third husband, John Smuts, she descended into poverty. She took on jobs as a janitor, a scrub woman, and a housekeeper. At the time of her death at the age of 72 in 1938, she was working as a clerk for the Works Progress Administration (WPA) earning $16.50 per week.

More than 3,000 people attended May's funeral that August and her husband, following her wishes, scattered her ashes in the Atlantic Ocean.

Since that time, May has returned to the place where she found the most happiness, the Bethlehem Hotel. To this day she gives impromptu performances in the lobby. The antique player piano located there is known to start up on its own, playing out favorites of yesteryear. Many people think she has something to do with that. Furthermore, she has made appearances on the third floor in the exercise room. And the smiling little girl who is seen beaming from random hotel windows sure resembles her description at an early age. [Could add some thoughts on whether ghosts can come back at different ages rather than just their age at death.]

Finally, there is Room 932, the Hotel Bethlehem's "room with a boo." People who have lodged overnight in that room have encountered many strange things. One couple was confronted by a man standing at the foot of their bed asking, "Why are you in my room?" When they turned on the light, he disappeared. Others have witnessed papers standing upright on the desk with no hands to hold them. Papers have also flown off the desk with no hands to throw them. Lamps in the room flash on, then off. At least one witness saw the wallpaper in the bathroom was turn pink, and numerous "orbs" have appeared in pictures taken in Room 932.

A paranormal investigator who overnighted in Room 932 came away with an armful of EVPs. Some of the statements recorded from unseen speakers: "I've locked myself in the closet." "Look out the window." "What a beautiful bathroom." "It's Mary."

If you want to stay in Room 932, you'd better book far in advance. It is probably the most popular room in the hotel.

Why not leave your car where it is and stroll along beautiful Main Street in the Historic District of this historic city? The next home of spectral citizens that we will visit is only a block away on the opposite side of the street.

The Sun Inn

566 Main Street
Bethlehem

On Christmas Eve 1741, the small community of Bethlehem was founded by Moravian missionaries on the banks of the Monocacy Creek in the colony of Pennsylvania. Seventeen years later the Sun Inn opened on Main Street. It was instantly regarded as one of the best places for weary travelers to get a good night's rest along with an abundant hot meal.

Many of our country's founding fathers chose the Sun Inn as their favored place to stay when in the area. George Washington and his wife, Martha; John Adams, and Ben Franklin made use of its facilities. The inn hosted "more signers of the Declaration of Independence than any other Inn," according to innkeeper and historian Bucky Szulborski.

In 1792, fifty-one chiefs and warriors of the Indian Nations stayed overnight at the inn on their way to a meeting with President Washington in Philadelphia. On their way back, they stayed again at the inn and signed a peace treaty that effectively ended the Indian unrest in the area.

In keeping with its popularity over the years, the Sun Inn grew and grew, with additions swallowing the original structure. Two additional floors were even erected over the first two-and-a-half stories.

Eventually, as time passed, the inn fell on hard times. Its rich history notwithstanding, it had become derelict by the middle of the 20th century. By the 1970s, the Sun Inn was scheduled for a meeting with the wrecker's ball.

But one person in Bethlehem was having none of that. An indefatigable and irrepressible dynamo who went by the name of Hughetta Bender organized the Sun Inn Association, devoted to the reclamation, restoration, and preservation of the Sun Inn. The association bought the property, raised additional funds, dug into Moravian archives to learn about the building's original structure, got the site listed on the National Register of Historic Places, and acquired funding.

The Sun Inn reopened in the summer of 1982 with most of the restoration complete. Hughetta watched over the results of her labors for another 13 years until her death at the age of 89. She was so satisfied with the work done there that her spirit stayed on after her mortal passing. A picture taken by a paranormal research group of a woman peering from a second-floor window was shown to Bucky Szulborski. He exclaimed, "Oh my God, that's Hughetta!" The image shows a gray-haired, bespectacled woman wearing a white apron, which was her trademark garb.

Hughetta is far from the only spirit at the inn, of course. During that same paranormal investigation in the winter of 2009, the Lehigh Valley-based group acquired more than fifteen separate unknown EVPs of what they thought was a ghostly party taking place in the dining room.

In 1897 a nurse by the name of Elizabeth Moore died at the inn. When a member of the group asked if Elizabeth was present, the reply "Moore," was heard on the recording. Another voice informed the investigators, "We are watching you."

The ghost of a young child inhabits the attic. It is thought to be Sarah, a girl who died on the premises. The sound of her trilling little singsong ditties comes through the walls from the attic. This lonely little girl begs visitors to the attic not to leave.

The ghost of an elderly gentleman observed sitting in a green chair by the fireplace in the Great Room was asked his name. On the EVP, he replied, "William." William Jones, President Madison's, Secretary of the Navy, died at the inn in 1831. Coincidence?

It seems that all these spirits approve of the restoration efforts of the Sun Inn Association and have no desire to vacate the premises in the foreseeable future.

Unfortunately, we have to vacate so that we can get to our next stop. Unless you are exceptionally energetic, you'll return to your car and head north on Main Street until you come to the beautiful, sprawling campus of Moravian College, just over a dozen blocks away.

Moravian College

Bethlehem

Soon after Bethlehem was named by the Moravians on Christmas Eve, 1741 they saw a need to educate their young ones. The following year they opened an all-girls boarding school in Bethlehem eventually called the Bethlehem Female Seminary. It quickly garnered such a reputation for excellence that President of the United States of America, George Washington, petitioned the headmaster of the school personally for the admission of two of his great-nieces. This was during his second term as president.

It was chartered by the Commonwealth of Pennsylvania to bestow baccalaureate degrees in 1863. In

1913, right before World War I, the institution of learning changed its name to the Moravian Seminary and College for Women.

A parallel school for young men was started in Bethlehem and nearby Nazareth in 1742 as well, also receiving a charter to grant baccalaureate degrees in 1863. Finally in 1954, over two centuries after they were founded, the two schools merged to become the Moravian College, a premier liberal arts institution, and the first coed college in the Lehigh Valley.

Along with all the tradition and history that this institution has accumulated over the years, it has accumulated its fair share of specters as well.

The Single Brethren's House built in 1748 was used for living space for unwed men now is the site of classrooms and offices for the Music Department. During the Revolutionary War it served as a hospital for wounded and recuperating Colonial soldiers. Some of those men died there and remained there ever after. This is evident from the abundance of paranormal activity in the building, including doors that open and slam shut on their own, spots that'll chill you to the point of goosebumps, and the tread of phantom footsteps. The phantom of a woman wearing a long flowing dress and a bonnet has been seen walking the grounds, appearing and disappearing randomly. She is thought to be one of the nurses that cared for the Colonial soldiers. The ghost of a dazed man was encountered by a custodian who described him as having both his head and arm wrapped in a bloody bandage.

Walking into Main Hall, built in 1854 and now used as student women's residence, you may notice an older couple quietly sitting on a couch enjoying each others company. If you try to engage them in conversation and they don't respond, it isn't because they are ignoring you. It's because they have long ago passed from mortality and are now spending eternity in the wonderful, comfortable love that comes to those who have grown old together.

Rau Hall, a dorm, was once the exclusive territory of female students. The basement of the place was less than inviting and those students living there named it "The Pit." Everybody is aware of the extremes of emotions felt by college students and the depth of despair that they may encounter over something that, in retrospect, may seem trivial to an outside observer. For whatever reason, college lore has it that three young coeds hung themselves down in that place known as The Pit. And now, perhaps they are ashamed to leave, because they are still there. The Pit is now inaccessible, except during the Rau's annual Halloween haunted house tour.

The South Campus is honeycombed with underground passages and tunnels. Some of these are said to have been used during the mid-1800s as way stations on the Underground Railroad for people escaping slavery. Recently they have been the source of unexplained banging so loud that classes have been disrupted by the noise.

Stately Comenius Hall was built in 1891 to house the entire men's college and seminary, including offices, classrooms, library, and dorms. Today, it is used for classrooms and faculty office space. Education pioneer Moravian Bishop John Amos Comenius is pleased with the building that bears his name and watches over the college from a vantage point on the top floor. He takes the appearance of a light that patrols that place.

Additionally, an unknown presence in the basement of the building is sufficient to cause canine anxiety in the form of raised hackles, but has been unseen by humans. Another spirit, this one of a World War One era soldier haunts the Hall. He has been seen throughout the building and is thought to be the ghost of a student who interrupted his education to serve in the army during that war. Unfortunately, he died in action and has returned to try to complete his education in the spiritual realm.

Alpha Sigma Tau sorority house on Main Street is the home of the ghost of a young lady who was first defiled, then disgraced and killed by the former master of the house when it was still a private mansion. Supposedly, a young maid in the house named Alicia was impregnated by the master of the house. When he learned of her pregnancy, instead of showing her the love that he had previously professed, he descended into a rage, denounced her, and threw her down a flight of stairs. She, along with her unborn child, died as a result of this treatment. Since that time, she has inhabited the attic that was also her quarters. People looking on the house from the outside have been treated to lights going on and off when nobody is home. Residents have been "treated" to lights going on and off in their bedrooms when nobody is near the switch. Pictures of male friends of the sorority sisters have been turned face down or covered. And she has taken it upon herself to protect the reputation of the young ladies who live there. On at least one occasion, when a young man attempted a sleepover, he and his lady friend were awakened in the middle of the night by a violently shaking bed and a frigid presence that chilled them to the bone.

A group of young men who decided to defy Alicia by

staying overnight in the attic found that their male bravado was no match for Alicia's ire. Supposedly, they fled in terror from the house at 2 in the morning vowing to never return again.

We have crossed and recrossed the Lehigh River a number of times. And now I want to tell you about an early occupant of Bethlehem and his reaction when some residents reported to him that they were being harassed by a ghost on the banks of that river.

Heckewelder's Ghost

**On the banks of the Lehigh River
Bethlehem, PA**

John Gottleib Ernestus Heckewelder was a man who was quite used to dealing with contentious folk. He was after all, the Moravian missionary who brought Christianity to the Lenni Lenape, or Delaware Indians. But long before he did that, he spent nearly a half-century as an evangelist to the Indians in what would later become the state of Ohio. His success led to his being twice commissioned to assist the government of the fledgling United States of America in its dealings and treaties with the Native Americans of the Great Lakes Region in present-day Ohio and Indiana.

After having his mettle tested in these endeavors, he served the people in the territory as a postmaster, a justice of the peace, and finally an associate justice in common pleas court. John Heckewelder had spent his entire life as a mediator of sorts, first as a bridge between common folk and the Almighty and then as an interpreter of the law of the land.

Finally, in 1810, at the age of 67, he retired to his home in Bethlehem to "engage in literary pursuits." For the next 13 years, John drew upon his vast knowledge of Native Americans, especially the Lenni Lenape, and published many papers and books about their customs and history that are considered definitive guides for archeologists and anthropologists to this very day.

Alas, his retirement was not without a bit of consternation. It fell upon John to dig into his repertoire of negotiating and mediation skills to settle a dispute between the realm of the living and that of the dead. Unlike Daniel Webster's set-to with the Devil, this one wasn't a fictional account. It's a short but true story, and here is how it goes:

In the early 1800s it was common practice for the farmers and townspeople of the Bethlehem area to lead their horses, cattle, goats, and sheep down to the banks of the Lehigh River to drink of the river's water and graze on the succulent grasses, bushes, and berries that grew along the shore.

Shortly after John Heckewelder arrived to enjoy his retirement in peace, that peace was interrupted when the townsfolk and their livestock were chased from the banks of the Lehigh River by a ghost. Upset cattle give poor-quality milk and upset neighbors are poor company, so John decided that something must be done. His negotiation skills were needed.

He proceeded to the bank of the Lehigh and

demanded an audience with the spirit who was causing such havoc. After a bit, when the ghost of a young woman appeared, he asked her why she was scaring off the people and animals who came to the riverbank. She answered his question with a story of her own.

She told him that she was the battered wife of a cruel husband from across the ocean. She had to escape his tyranny, but she had a child and didn't have the resources to travel with it. To prevent the child from falling into the clutches of her cruel husband, she drowned it and fled to America, coming finally to Bethlehem. But she was unable to make a new life here because the enormity of what she had done overcame her. The remorse was more than she could bear, so she drowned herself, just as she had done with her child.

Her punishment for infanticide was to roam the banks of the Lehigh River near Bethlehem until her natural time to die arrived. Then, and only then, would she be permitted to leave this world for the hereafter. She was just a poor, distraught young thing who had no intention to scare anyone. She was no evil haunt. She just wanted to be left alone.

John Heckewelder returned to town and explained the predicament of the poor spirit. The folk returned to grazing their livestock on the riverbanks, secure in the knowledge that she meant them no harm. The townsfolk, their livestock, and the ghost of the riverbank coexisted so peacefully that, when her time was served and she crossed over, nobody took notice.

John Heckewelder himself passed over to the hereafter at 6:00 in the morning on January 31, 1823, at the age of 79 years. Perhaps he then met the young ghost of the riverbank under more congenial circumstances.

Starting back at Moravian College, a short ride will take us to another Christmas town, Nazareth, nine miles away. Head east on Elizabeth Avenue until you get to Linden Street. Turn left on Linden Street and just keep on going. Linden Street becomes the Nazareth-Bethlehem Pike and PA Route 191, taking you into the heart of this town. Follow PA Route 191 right through Nazareth. When it turns right onto Walnut Street keep going on Broad Street, and you will come to Nazareth Boro Park, our next stop.

Ed Kelemen

~VI~

Eastern Pennsylvania

The Indian Tower

Nazareth Boro Park
211 North Broad Street Extension
Nazareth

Near the Indian Tower are three bronze plaques that tell the story of how it came to be.

The first plaque tells how the borough of Nazareth itself was created. It is titled "The Barony of The Rose" and is inscribed, "The rose's significance to Nazareth dates back to when Letitia Penn Aubrey was given 5,000 acres of land by her father, William Penn. The only payment necessary for the land was one rose to be delivered to her father on the 24th day of June each year. The original 5,000 acres included the borough of

Nazareth and Upper Nazareth Township, and they became known as the Barony of the Rose."

The next plaque is simply titled "The Indian Graveyard." It says, "This is the site of Nazareth's first Moravian graveyard, called "God's Acre," in use from 1744 to 1762. It is erroneously thought to be the burial ground of the Indians from the nearby village of Welagamika, but there are only 4 Indians buried here. Robert Haas created this American marble monument, dedicated by the American Moravian Historical Society in 1867, at the same time the original pavilion was constructed. This monument is inscribed with the names of the 67 Moravians, including the four Indians, who are buried here."

Finally, the third plaque is titled "The Indian Tower." It explains how the tower came by its name: "The Indian Tower sits at the highest point of the original 5,000 acres of Nazareth. The original structure was a pavilion called "The Summer House," built in 1867 by John Jordan Jr. He later donated $200 to the Moravian Historical Society to replace the pavilion with the present-day tower, which was completed in 1916. The Indian Tower is commonly thought to have been used as a lookout for hostile Indians, but in actuality, the Indians had been forcibly removed from Pennsylvania long before the tower was built. It received its name because of the Indian graveyard it overlooks. This tower has been used for many purposes over the years: as a Civil Defense lookout during WWII, as a repeater station for emergency services, and always to rest and reflect."

Visitors to this now graffiti-plagued site encounter shadowy figures roaming the tower and hear footfalls of unseen people ringing on the steps to the top. Unwanted visitors are told by a semitransparent figure, "Let my people go." It is assumed that the spirit is a spokesman for the dead who populate the area and just want to be left alone. Some people are simply told, "Go away." If you have the fortitude to ignore these warnings and climb the steps to the top of the tower, you will be rewarded with an unobstructed view of the nearby cemetery, where shadowy forms roam the graves.

After stretching our legs and maybe enjoying a cup of coffee while walking in the park, we'll get in our car and drive back into Nazareth on Broad Street. Turn left onto East Center Street, stopping at house number 214, the Whitefield House.

The Whitefield House

214 East Center Street
Nazareth

Another Moravian building dating back to 1743! The second floor of this beautifully gabled stone structure was used as a combination nursery, school, and residence for children of Nazareth and Bethlehem from 1749 to 1764. It must have resounded with their joyful cries as they played, studied, and learned hymns. Unfortunately, there was also sadness during that time; as smallpox epidemics swept the area, resulting in many deaths. Most of the 70 children buried in the cemetery near the Indian Tower died while residing at the Whitefield House.

The business manager of the Whitefield House Museum shares an experience. One day, while walking up to the second floor of the museum, she saw a woman descending the stairs. She thought nothing of it, assuming that she was a visitor to the museum. Then she realized that the woman was wearing period dress of the type worn by the Moravian nurses who staffed the children's nursery. Turning around, the business manager saw the woman simply disappear, but she felt no fear, knowing of the peaceful, caring attributes of the Moravian nurses.

Another staff member felt such strong vibes when ascending to the third floor that she couldn't even reach the top of the steps. She felt a strong male presence who told her that his name was Henry.

A paranormal group conducting an investigation of the premises used a device called a trigger object, an item placed where spirits can interact with it, thereby confirming their presence. Some items commonly used as trigger objects are talc, wind chimes, and pendulums. In this instance, the spirit of a small girl was felt to be present, so a tennis ball was used. It was placed on one of the pews in the chapel. The museum staffer who accompanied the paranormal investigators saw the ball rise up in the air, bounce on the pew, and roll away. No child has ever been able to resist playing with a ball.

The house's propensity for the supernatural isn't new. Way back when it was being used as a nursery/school/residence, the children spent a restless night one time, complaining to their nurses about hearing footsteps, whispered conversations, and groaning in the hallway outside their sleeping spaces. The following day, a messenger arrived on horseback after riding through the night to tell of an Indian raid on a mission house in Lehighton, 26 miles to the northwest. Several of the missionaries had been murdered. The children somehow heard their dying cries.

All right now. Take a trip around the block and turn back down Broad Street. Retrace our earlier route by turning right on Easton Road, then left onto the Nazareth-Bethlehem Pike (Route 191). Half mile or so along the road is the intersection with Newburg Road. It is also our next stop, the Newburg Inn. What better place to have lunch on a tour of haunted places than a haunted tavern?

The Newburg Inn

4357 Newburg Rd.
Nazareth

The Newburg Inn was built on property originally owned by the founder and namesake of Pennsylvania, William Penn in 1750. This was after the property had been deeded to William Penn's sons, John and Richard.

The inn first served as a Trading post where the original proprietor dealt trade goods with the local Indian tribes in exchange for furs, pelts and other items of value. This was a relatively short-lived use of the property, since it was located at a crossroads that soon served stagecoach lines running between Philadelphia,

Harrisburg, and New York City. It became into a stagecoach stop where travelers could rest overnight, get a good meal, enjoy convivial company and drinks, and be protected from marauders such as highwaymen and Indians. Evidence of this use lies in the roof hatch still on the roof that could, and still can, be raised offering sharpshooters a vantage point when those raids occurred.

The inn's popularity required that the original structure be enlarged in 1802 and again in 1941 to its present-day configuration. Today, this historic landmark is a fine dining establishment that shares its rich history with a number of phantasms who make their presence known in a variety of ways.

The owner's office phone receives some really long distance calls. You see, he has rushed to answer it, only to find that it wasn't even plugged in. Needless to say, the caller didn't bother to identify himself. Nobody ever asked him if the caller ID said, "Afterlife." He has also been treated to the sounds of footsteps treading on the roof above his head when there obviously wasn't anyone of substance there. One of the wait staff nearly tripped over a dark and shapeless figure that crossed her path, and observed a diaphanous figure float through the barroom another time.

Another employee has experienced disembodied footsteps, overheard conversations between unseen people, and has even held a discussion with one of the inn's ghosts.

Finally, the owner related an incident that happened one night at closing time. As he was locking up, he noticed a large apparition standing beside him observing his actions.

Well, of course all this activity attracted the attention

of paranormal investigators. The City Lights Paranormal Society, with the permission of the owner, conducted an investigation at the inn. The City Lights Paranormal Society is one which, according to their website, is dedicated to, "proving/disproving claims of activity through compassionate yet skeptical studies of all our cases." They came away with numerous EVPs, personal experiences, and even photographs of manifestations, overcoming their skepticism, and allowing them to state that, "Yes, the Newburg Inn is HAUNTED."

Leaving here, head on down to Route 22 and head east for the final time. Take the 4th Street Exit in Easton, PA and turn right onto Spring Garden Street that becomes West Street. Then a right onto West Street will bring us to the Easton Public Library. And guess what it is built upon?

The Easton Library

**515 Church Street
Easton**

Here we go again! Another library built over a cemetery! When are people going to learn? Back around the turn of the 20th century, steel baron Andrew Carnegie offered up $50,000 to build a library in Easton if the town fathers could provide a location for it. What did they choose? An abandoned cemetery. And it must've been just too much trouble to find and rebury elsewhere all the bodies that had been interred there because it was reported that "most of the bodies were relocated." That is, all but 30 of the 514 souls who had their earthly remains committed to that blessed soil. The rest, along with miscellaneous body parts and pieces of coffins that had been unearthed during construction, were unceremoniously dumped together in a common vault that today is located under a depression in the parking lot. What a final "resting" place.

Two of the deceased, William Parsons and Elizabeth Bell Morgan, received better treatment due to their fame and popularity during Easton's early days. William Parsons was a surveyor who helped lay out the original design of the city of Easton. His grave site was relocated to a spot near the main entrance to the library.

Elizabeth Morgan, known affectionately as "Mammy Morgan" during and after her life, was a beloved innkeeper in Easton who was twice widowed. Her first husband was a Revolutionary War soldier named Hugh Bay who died shortly after their marriage. The Widow Bay then met and married Philadelphia physician Abel Morgan, who also was deeply interested in the legal profession. In the late 1790s, Abel died and Mammy Morgan inherited his vast law library. She made this collection of legal papers and books available to all who came to her Williams Township hotel. Until her death in 1839, Mammy Morgan's was the go-to place for legal advice for those who couldn't afford it as well as those who could.

Mammy Morgan is reburied on the west lawn of the library grounds. Her grave is marked with an Indian grindstone, which was placed there by the Northampton County Historical and Genealogical Society. Over the years, Mammy has been seen to leave the confines of her grave and wander the grounds, but no reports exist on whether or not she has dispensed any legal advice to those she encounters.

Inside the library itself, patrons and employees alike have experienced invisible hands running through their hair. Others receive taps on the shoulder. When they turn around to answer the tap, they find themselves alone.

Doors slam shut, then just as quickly open, unaided by earthly denizens. Cabinet drawers roll out with no warning, causing people to bump into them.

All in all, these occurrences are relatively benign responses to the disrespect with which the dearly departed were treated on those cold days in 1903.

Just around the block on Northampton Street is the world-famous State Theater, which is home to its own lovable haunt.

State Theater

453 Easton Street
Easton

The State Theater is more than a gem of a performing arts center. It is a royal crown of sparkling jewels. It was built as the Northampton National Bank Building in 1873. The original facade has been preserved, and a teller's cage serves as the ticket booth.

In 1910 the bank was no more, and a small theater named the Neumeyer opened on the spot. From 1914 to

1916 it changed names from the Neumeyer to the Northampton Theater, then the Colonial Theater.

Finally in 1926 the great State Theater was born on that same spot with its present-day configuration. It saw unprecedented popularity as a vaudeville emporium, once playing host to 5,000 patrons in one day. Its popularity didn't diminish when Hollywood entered the golden age of moving pictures. Its actors continued to play to full houses for 30 years. During the 1970s, the State Theater was home to numerous rock concerts. But then it fell on hard times, facing demolition in 1981.

With the impetus furnished by a group called Friends of the State Theater and a $20,000 infusion of funds from the city of Easton, the State Theater escaped its fate. Fifteen years and $3.7 million later, this grand old dame was back, better than ever.

Headliners in all genres of theater from all over the world have performed on its stage for audiences that routinely reach over one hundred thousand people per year.

This was all accomplished under the watchful eye of J. Fred Osterstock, who managed the facility that he so loved from 1936 until he died in 1965. Freddy even lived inside the theater when the first floor of his house was under water for several weeks during the floods of 1955. His office, just off the theater's foyer, was also his home during that time.

Freddy was so attached to his beloved theater that he couldn't bring himself to leave, even after death. He started making his presence known during the 1970s. A well-dressed man was spotted in storage rooms and seen roaming the building. One time the police were called to intercept the trespasser, but they found nobody of substance in the theater. Their K-9 partners, however, bristled at something unseen.

Finally the elusive occupant of the State Theater was identified. While closing up for the night one evening in the late 1970s, historian Ken Klabunde saw someone walk from the supposedly empty stage. He later identified the person he saw as J. Fred Osterstock from a photograph.

Since then, Freddy has been seen in one of the boxes, on the stage, and throughout the building. His spirit has been adopted by staff, management, performers, and audiences as a patron and is welcomed with opened arms. The theater's annual awards ceremony honoring outstanding high school theatrical achievement in the Lehigh Valley has been named the Freddy Awards after him.

The theater's annual awards ceremony honoring outstanding high school theatrical achievement in the Lehigh Valley has been named the Freddy Awards after him.

Next up is not quite as benign a haunt as Freddy. We will track an irascible murder's last corporeal existence to an island named after him. Head east down and around the town square. Turn left at the traffic signal just in front of the bridge and follow PA Route 611 along the bank of the Delaware River. Go under U.S. Route 22 and observe that little wooded island to your right. At least one criminal found justice there.

Getter's Island

Delaware River
Easton

Bisecting the Delaware River just north of the Route 22 bridge crossing over into New Jersey is a wooded strip of land innocuously named Getter's Island. It has another, less sanitized name: Hangman's Island.

But, our story doesn't start at the island, it ends there. You see, the ghost of a young lady by the name of Margaret Lawall-Getter haunts the Northampton Country Club a couple miles west of the river. She roams the grounds of the country club, giving pause to golfers when she appears blissfully unaware of their cries of "Fore!"

Poor Margaret was murdered there when it was still the site of a quarry that existed to provide building stones for area construction. In 1833, when Carl Getter was a young randy lad of 25 working as a farmhand in nearby Forks Township, the 31-year old Margaret identified him as the father of her unborn child. Dragged in front of the local justice of the peace, Carl opted to do the honorable thing. He avoided jail by marrying Margaret.

As things transpired, Carl discovered that he held no affection for Margaret beyond their one fateful encounter, stated that he didn't even like her, and refused to live with her. Carl was not one to bank the first of his passion and, by-and-by, he fell under the charm of another young local lady more to his liking. Her name was Molly Hummer and Carl vowed to make her his wife. But there was an obstacle to the consummation of their ardor. That obstacle was Margaret. That obstacle had to be removed, so the love-stricken Carl took things into his own hands, strangled her and dumped her body in the quarry.

When Margaret's body was discovered, it didn't take a Mensa Member to figure out whodunnit. Carl was arrested, tried, and sentenced to be hanged.

The hanging took place on that strip of land in the middle of the Delaware River on February 28, 1833. It was such a spectacle, that the militia had to be called out to maintain order and control the tens of thousands of people who converged on Easton to witness the hanging.

Now, this was to be no ordinary hanging where the condemned man drops through a trap door in the scaffolding until the rope achieves tension based on his body weight and thusly kills him either by strangulation(poetic justice in this case), or by breaking his neck. Nope, it was done, "New York Style."

In this manner of execution, the condemned man

stands with the noose around his neck attached to a rope above him. That rope is then run through a series of pulleys and finally terminates in a heavy weight. When the weight is dropped, the condemned man's body is yanked from his feet by the rope and he expires at the end of that rope. In theory.

In Carl's case, it didn't go as planned. On the first try, the rope jerked him up about three feet in to the air then broke, dumping him on the platform. It stunned him and he lay there for a minute or two getting his wind back. Then he looked up with a smirking smile on his face and sneered, "That was good for nothing."

The second rope performed better and the execution was successful. A length of the rope used to hang Carl Getter is now on display at the Northampton County Historical Society at 342 Northampton Street in Easton.

Since that date, perhaps because he was dissatisfied with the turn of events that caused his execution to deteriorate into a comedy of errors, or as punishment for his murderous deed, Carl roams the Island that has been named after him, trapped there by the running water of the Delaware River for eternity.

And now we come to our last stop on our haunted trip along Pennsylvania's stretch of U.S. Route 22. Turn around on Route 611 and follow it back, cross under Route 22 and keep heading south crossing the Lehigh River and following the bank of the Delaware River. Let's visit a gangster's final hideout.

Stemie's/Black Horse Inn

831 South Delaware Drive
on PA Route 611
Easton

What better place to end our cross-state trip than at a haunted historical site that has been in business for over two and a half centuries? You can sit comfortably at a window overlooking the Delaware River, just as westward-heading settlers did in the 1780s. And while you're at it, you can rub elbows with a mob boss who met his end on these very premises.

Let's go back a few years – to 1783. That year saw an incredible increase in pioneers heading west to settle the newly formed United States of America. And the ferry at the crossing on the Delaware River at Easton was how they headed in that direction, thousands upon thousands of them. The city grew by leaps and bounds, and many mercantile shops were formed to serve the population, both permanent and transient.

The Black Horse Tavern was built on the bank of the

river in that year to offer food and lodging to those who traveled through Easton as well as to those who lived here. Over the years it evolved to meet the needs and wants of its patrons. It saw life as a tavern, a stagecoach stop, and a canal-boat stop. For some reason, from the day it opened its doors it attracted a less than savory clientele. In fact, the whole town gained a reputation as a place of questionable character where "anything goes." During the 1800s, the Black Horse was a place where ladies of the night were available, as well as games of chance.

When Prohibition arrived, the Black Horse became a speakeasy where mob bosses and their minions congregated to conduct business. As the booze flowed, business was conducted and contracts were awarded.

One connected person who was a habitué of the Black Horse was a gentleman by the name of Savario Damiano. Yet he went by the name of Johnny "the Wop" Ferrara. During the summer of 1928 Johnny was supposedly lying low in Easton. He was what we would call today "a person of interest" in the killing of a Philadelphia physician. But apparently his lifestyle at the Black Horse wasn't conducive to blending in.

On July 28 of that year, Johnny was engaged in a telephone conversation with an associate, Sam Scalleat. It was around 9:00 p.m. and was the end of another hazy, hot, and humid day by the river. The windows were open to catch what breeze they could. Between his conversation with Sam and the background conversation and music in the tavern, Johnny probably didn't hear the crunch of tires on gravel as the car pulled into the lot.

Suddenly four mobsters equipped with shotguns and pistols kicked their way through the front door, spotted

Johnny the Wop on the phone, and opened fire. Both his conversation and his life came to an abrupt end. Johnny was hit several times but still tried to escape, stumbling down the stairs to the basement. The hit men followed him, pumping bullets into his body as he crawled across the basement floor, finally coming to a stop some twenty feet from the bottom of the stairs.

One of the gunmen stood over his body and delivered the *coup de grace* into the back of Johnny's head, commenting, "Well, I guess he's had enough." He was wrong.

For a while, the Black Horse lay dormant. It reopened in 2002 as Stemies. The new owners not only took possession of a historic restaurant, they also became Johnny's new landlords.

That's because, regardless of where his body was interred, his spirit never left. Johnny has stayed on as a playful ghost. He taps people on the shoulder, moves food around in the kitchen, tosses serving trays, calls people by name when no one else is about, and pushes the ladies room door open, startling unfortunate occupants. A male entity assumed to be Johnny is seen flitting here and there in the Tavern, and his shadowy presence turns up in photos taken on the premises.

Over the last few years, Johnny has been joined by a former waitress who was so severely beaten that she died in the arms of one of the owners at her home. She was a close friend of the owners, and they have felt her presence many times since her passing. One patron reported that the waitress appeared in a dream and said, "I'm back."

As you sit there contemplating our long journey across the state, sit back, relax, and realize that not all of the entertainment at Stemies is necessarily "live" entertainment.

And now our 300-plus mile journey along the many paths that U.S. Route 22 takes across Pennsylvania has come to an end. I sincerely hope you have enjoyed sharing your trip with those who have had their trips to the Great Beyond interrupted and who have remained in our world for whatever reason.

Visiting The Ghosts of Route 22

Maybe you may want to do more than just read about the haunted places along Route 22. You may want to visit them and maybe experience the hair standing up on the back of your neck, goosebumps, and cold chills associated with interacting with otherworldly denizens.

So, in this section I am listing all the contact information I have for those places that are open to the public or commercial in nature. One caveat- this information is correct at press time. Things change. Do yourself a favor and verify any information in this section before visiting them. Also, some of these places are seasonal in nature and it would be disappointing to show up there, only to find out that it is closed.

For your convenience, I will list them in the order in which they appear in the book.

Point State Park
101 Commonwealth Place #1
Pittsburgh, PA. 15222
(412)471-0235
www.dcnr.state.pa.us/stateparks/findapark/point
www.fortpittblockhouse.com

Heinz History Center
1212 Smallman Street
Pittsburgh, PA 15222
(412)454-6000
www.heinzhistorycenter.org

Church Brew Works
3525 Liberty Avenue
Pittsburgh, PA 15201
www.churchbrew.com
(412)688-8200

Carnegie Library of Pittsburgh
Lawrenceville Branch
279 Fisk Street
Pittsburgh, PA 15201
(412)682-3668
www.carnegielibrary.org/.../lawrenceville

Childrens Hospital of Pittsburgh of UPMC
4401 Penn Avenue
Pittsburgh, PA 15224
(412)692-5325
www.chp.edu/

Frick Art and Historical Center
Clayton
7227 Reynolds Street
Pittsburgh, PA 15208
(412)371-0600
www.thefrickpittsburgh.org/start/venues/clayton.php

New Alexandria
www.newalex.com

The Ghost Town Trail
www.indianacountyparks.org/trails/gtt/gtt.html

Eliza Furnace
Main Street
Vintondale, PA 15931
www.indianacountyparks.org/parks/ef/ef.html

Lemon House at the
Allegheny Portage Railroad National Historic Site
110 Federal Park Rd.
Gallitizin, PA 16641
(814)886-6150
www.nps.gov/alpo/

Bennington Curve ghosts at the
Gallitzin Tunnels
Gallitzin Tunnels Park and Museum
DeGol Plaza
411 Convent Street, Suite 20
Gallitzin, PA 16641
(8147)886-8871
www.gallitzin.info/index.php

The Horseshoe Curve
Kittanning Point Road
Altoona, PA 16601
(814)946-0834
www.railroadcity.com/visit/world-famous-horseshoe-curve/

The Mishler Theater
1208 125th Avenue #206
Altoona, PA 16601
(814)944-9434
mishlertheater.org

Railroaders Memorial Museum
1300 9th Avenue
Altoona, PA 16602
(814)946-0834
www.railroadcity.com

Baker Mansion
Blair County Historical Society
3419 Oak Lane
Altoona, PA 16602
(814)942-3916
www.blairhistory.org

Lakemont Park and the Island Water Park
700 Park Avenue
Altoona, PA 16602
(814)949-7275
www.lakemontpark.com

Royer Mansion
3909 Piney Creek Road
Williamsburg, PA 16693
(814)381-3388 & 942-3916
www.blairhistory.org

The Inn at Edgewater Acres
7653 Edgewater Acres
Alexandria, PA 16611
(814)669-4144
www.edgewateracres.net

Hawk Mountain Sanctuary
1700 Hawk Mountain Road
Kempton, PA 19529
(610)765-6961
www.hawkmountain.org

The Inn at Maple Grove
2165 State Street
Alburtis, PA 18011
(610)682-4346
www.innatmaplegroveinc.com

Dorney Park
3830 Dorney Park Road
Allentown, PA 18104
(610)395-3724
www.dorneypark.com

The Roxy Theater
2004 Main Street
Northampton, PA 18067
(610)262-7699
www.roxytheaternorthampton.com

Moravian Book Shop
428 Main Street
Bethlehem, PA 18018
(610)866-5481
www.moravianbookshop.com

Hotel Bethlehem
437 Main Street
Bethlehem, PA 18/018
(610)625-5000
www.hotelbethlehem.com

Sun Inn
556 Main Street #2
Bethlehem, PA 18018
(484)821-0809
www.suninnbethlehem.org

The Indian Tower at Nazareth Borough Park
Broad Street Extension
Nazareth, PA 18064
(610)759-3522
www.nazareth.patch.com/listing/nazareth-boro-park

Whitefield House
Headquarters of the Moravian Historical Society
214 East Center Street
Nazareth, PA 18064
(610)759-5070
www.moravianhistoricalsociety.org

Newburg Inn
4357 Newburg Road
Nazareth, PA 18064
(610)759-8528
www.newburginn.com

Easton Area Public Library
515 Church Street
Easton, PA 18042
(610)258-2917
www.eastlonpl.org

State Theater
453 Northampton Street
Easton, PA 18042
(610)252-3132
statetheater.org

Stemie's Place/Black Horse Inn
831 S. Delaware Drive
Easton, PA 18042
(610)253-2700
No Web Site

ABOUT THE AUTHOR

Ed Kelemen is a writer, columnist, and playwright who lives in a small West Central Pennsylvania town with his wife, two of five sons, a pair of humongous dogs and a clutch of attitude-ridden cats. His article and short stories have appeared in numerous local, regional, and national publications. Visit with him at www.ekelemen.com.

Other Books by Ed Kelemen

~Pennsylvania's Haunted Route 30~
A haunted road trip across Pennsylvania along the Lincoln Highway, the nation's first coast-to-coast road.

~We Don't Talk About Those Kinds of Things - The Making of a Psychic~
Written with Bev LaGorga, join her on her odyssey from a confused little girl who "sees things" to an adult woman who helps people who are having problems with spirits and other paranormal phenomena.

~The Little Drummer Girl of Gettysburg~
Abby has haunted Gettysburg ever since she was mistakenly buried as a Confederate soldier. It is up to four youngsters from Pittsburgh on vacation to rectify her situation. A wonderful middle grade novel.

All of these books can be ordered through your local bookstore and are available at Amazon.com.

Made in the USA
Middletown, DE
11 July 2015